DESIGN THINKING

DESIGN THINKING IN CONSULTING

MOHAN KANCHARLA

INDIA • SINGAPORE • MALAYSIA

Notion Press Media Pvt Ltd

No. 50, Chettiyar Agaram Main Road,
Vanagaram, Chennai, Tamil Nadu – 600 095

First Published by Notion Press 2021
Copyright © Mohan Kancharla 2021
All Rights Reserved.

ISBN
Hardcase: 978-1-63904-631-7
Paperback: 978-1-63781-637-0

This book has been published with all efforts taken to make the material error-free after the consent of the author. However, the author and the publisher do not assume and hereby disclaim any liability to any party for any loss, damage, or disruption caused by errors or omissions, whether such errors or omissions result from negligence, accident, or any other cause.

While every effort has been made to avoid any mistake or omission, this publication is being sold on the condition and understanding that neither the author nor the publishers or printers would be liable in any manner to any person by reason of any mistake or omission in this publication or for any action taken or omitted to be taken or advice rendered or accepted on the basis of this work. For any defect in printing or binding the publishers will be liable only to replace the defective copy by another copy of this work then available.

DEDICATED TO

My Parents **Late Mangaiah Kancharla** and
Late Satyavedam Kancharla who often said
"Education is the only Inheritance we can give You".
Amma, Nanna that you have given me aplenty,
this book is a fruit of your labor.

Contents

Prologue *9*

Part One | Consulting

1. Consulting Retrospective 15
2. 'Mystery' of Consulting.. 45

Part Two | Design Thinking

3. Design Thinking Perspective 53
4. 'Heuristic' of Design Thinking.. 75

Part Three | Design Thinking in Consulting

5. 'Algorithm' for Design Thinking in Consulting........................ 99
6. Design Thinking in Understanding Context 103
7. Design Thinking in Current State Assessment 123
8. Design Thinking in Target State Definition 143
9. Design Thinking in Analysis and Findings 165
10. Design Thinking in Report and Recommendations 185

Bibliography.. *201*
End Notes *203*
Epilogue.. *205*
Index *207*
About the Author.. *209*

Prologue

In "**Consulting | A Practitioner's Perspective**", I have introduced readers to the world of IT Consulting, focusing on the individual, the practitioner. In a systematic and structured way, the book skillfully unfolds the science behind the art of consulting. Consulting Basics introduced the basics of consulting – consulting space, consulting cycle, and consulting frameworks. Consulting Spectrum detailed each segment of the IT Consulting Spectrum – Strategy, Architecture, Portfolio, Process, Governance, Infrastructure, Outsourcing, and Transformation in terms of their context, concepts, components, approach, frameworks, and guiding principles. Consulting Competencies highlighted the competencies required for consulting sales, proposals, execution, analysis, presenting findings, and reporting recommendations; collectively they serve as a comprehensive guide to succeeding in the IT consulting space.

The next logical question in my mind, and presumably in every reader's mind would be – How to sustain this success? Directed my research to contemporary thought on what would work in the future – a world in which enterprises would be embracing digital technologies and end-users would be demanding enhanced customer experience. Strange as it may sound, I found my answer in Design Thinking. I say strange because, design thinking in products is proven, design thinking in services is evolving, design thinking in consulting is radical. But then, "Design is not just what it looks like and feels like, Design is how it works." – Steve Jobs.

So, what is Design Thinking? Design Thinking is a human-centered approach to innovation that draws from the designer's toolkit to integrate the needs of people, the possibilities of technology, and the requirements for business success. Design thinking relies on our ability to be intuitive, recognize patterns, and construct ideas that have emotional meaning as well as functionality. Design thinking has an amalgamation of approaches; this is still quite unique, which is why sometimes design thinking is applied as more of an umbrella term. The approach I chose for design thinking is by constructing the Design Grid, a combination of Principles that are applied by diverse People as a set of Practices to solve a wide range of Problems.

And now, how design thinking can be applied to consulting? Let's explore a new way of thinking – Roger Martin's 'Knowledge Funnel'. The first stage of the funnel is a 'Mystery', in this case consulting in the context of design thinking. In the second stage, the mystery is worked down to manageable use, the 'Heuristic', an organized exploration of possibilities, the principles, and practices of design thinking. The third stage is 'Algorithm', converting general rules of thumb to fixed formulae that provide an explicit step by step method for people to solve the problem.

In three parts, this book builds upon the above three stages to evaluate consulting, explore design thinking, and extrapolate design thinking in consulting.

Chapter 1	Consulting Retrospective, re-visits the elements of the Consulting Space, segments of the Consulting Spectrum, and phases of the Consulting Cycle to re-understand Consulting.
Chapter 2	'Mystery' of Consulting, explains the knowledge funnel and applies the same to consulting for exploring the mysteries of consulting, which can be addressed by leveraging Design Thinking.
Chapter 3	Design Thinking Perspective, introduces design thinking in terms of evolution, definitions, elements, and application to business, plus frameworks to fully comprehend Design Thinking.
Chapter 4	'Heuristic' of Consulting, evaluates mysteries of consulting and explores the possibilities for design thinking in consulting. The emergent pattern is the design grid – a matrix of principles and practices of design thinking.

Chapter 5	'Algorithm' for Design Thinking in Consulting, evaluates the principles and practices of design thinking applicable to consulting and enhances the design grid for each phase of the consulting cycle.
Chapter 6	Design Thinking in Understanding Context, extrapolates the principles and practices of design thinking applicable to understanding context and highlighting the nuances pertinent for select segments.
Chapter 7	Design Thinking in Current State Assessment, extrapolates the principles and practices of design thinking applicable to current state assessment and highlighting the nuances pertinent for select segments.
Chapter 8	Design Thinking in Target State Definition, extrapolates the principles and practices of design thinking applicable to target state definition and highlighting the nuances for select segments.
Chapter 9	Design Thinking in Analysis & Findings, extrapolates the principles and practices of design thinking applicable to analysis & findings, and highlighting the nuances pertinent for select segments.
Chapter 10	Design Thinking in Report & Recommendations, extrapolates the principles and practices of design thinking applicable to report & recommendations and highlighting the nuances pertinent for select segments.

Lastly, let me express my sincere gratitude to my parents, who have bestowed upon me the greatest asset – education, to all my teachers who shaped my learning, to all my managers who taught me to think on my feet, to all my mentors who encouraged me to think out of the box, to all my colleagues who challenged every hypothesis, to all my clients who constantly raised the bar of perfection, to my readers whose critique compelled me to reflect and to my wife my greatest critic, to my daughters my inspiration, and above all to the Lord Almighty.

It's NOT my Merit... but HIS Grace!

Part One
Consulting

Chapter 1

Consulting Retrospective

Consulting – A Practitioner's Perspective[1], is a beginner's guide to the world of consulting, for firms planning to create a footprint and for fellow professionals aiming to get a foothold in this fascinating space. The book presents a comprehensive collection of practitioners' insights compiled from experiences ranging from practice creation, consultative selling, offering development, execution of engagements, building competencies, and mentoring consultants. Perspectives covered are across the consulting spectrum from strategy to architecture, portfolio, process, governance, infrastructure, outsourcing, and transformation consulting.

An in-depth understanding of the Consulting competencies, Consulting space, Consulting firms, Consulting market, Consulting cycle, Consulting frameworks, including scope, drivers, applicable framework's and approaches to executing engagements for each of the segments in the IT Consulting spectrum is a pre-requisite to succeed in the IT Consulting space.

The key stakeholder in the above is the 'Client', whose ask gets addressed by the recommendations of the 'Consultant'. While this yeilds results at a given point of time, the real test is the implications of implementation and experiences of the end-user over a period of time. The end-user here is the client and client's customers, the extended stakeholders. Therefore, the additional dimensions to be addressed by consultants to sustain success in the IT Consulting space are extended stakeholders over an extended period. Thus, there is a need for understanding

---

1 Kancharla, M. (2016), *Consulting – A Practitioner's Perspective,* Notion Press.

customer experiences and adopting a human-centered approach to problem-solving; one such approach is 'Design Thinking'.

In this chapter, elements of the Consulting Space, segments of the Consulting Spectrum, and phases of the Consulting Cycle are summarized to re-understand consulting.

Consulting Space

Elements of the Consulting space are Strategy consulting, Business consulting, Functional consulting, IT consulting, and Operations consulting. A brief overview of each element is given below:

1. ### Strategy Consulting

   Strategy consulting firms focus on direction setting and operate only at the CEO or Board level, where the advisory is by invitation. Firms and consultants in this space demonstrate high levels of maturity, positioning highly customized propositions with a high degree of complexity in execution.

   Typical engagements would be market entry strategies, competitive positioning of products, mergers & acquisitions, etc. Turnaround time is limited but expectations are high, necessitating the participation of experienced partners. The outcomes are a set of strategic directions requiring board approval, which upon implementation should enhance value to the business and the shareholders.

2. ### Business Consulting

   Business consulting firms focus on business outcomes aligned with the defined corporate strategy. The offerings of such firms are strategy-focused and their consultants are capable of solving complex business problems. Customers are typically CEOs.

   Typical engagements are market growth strategies, studies to enhance customer service, improve time to market, etc. Timeframes are short to medium and would require experienced subject matter experts. The end deliverable is a business strategy document that defines a set of priority initiatives that are required to achieve the desired business outcome, along with a business case.

3. **FUNCTIONAL CONSULTING**

Functional consulting firms focus either on a particular function in organizations or an industry in general, hence are also called domain consulting firms. The space in which functional consulting firms operate is a niche, requiring their consultants to be very strong in their industry domain. The buyers are the respective functional chiefs [CXOs].

Best examples of functional consulting engagements are performance and pay policy definition, financial re-engineering in banks, regulatory compliance in insurance companies, etc. Timeframes are short to medium and would require experienced functional experts. The end deliverable is an assessment report that establishes the current state and initiatives required to reach the target state or course corrections required to achieve compliance.

4. **IT CONSULTING**

The focus of IT consulting firms is on the technology of business and the business of technology. IT consulting firms operate in the region where IT intersects business. IT consultants are technology savvy and business-oriented. Customers of their offerings are mostly CIOs.

IT consulting engagements include strategy, governance, portfolio management, architecture, and transformation consulting all in the technology domain. Timeframes are medium to long and would require experienced technology and subject matter experts. The end deliverable is a consulting report that outlines alignment to business strategy and/or a roadmap of technology initiatives that can deliver business value.

5. OPERATIONAL CONSULTING

Operational consulting firms focus on operational efficiency in business operations. The offerings are related to monitoring, measuring, and management of operations. Consultants are seasoned managers experienced in operations.

Consulting engagements in the purview of operational consulting are business process outsourcing, application/infrastructure outsourcing analysis, process optimization, program management, change management, etc. Timeframes are long and would require hands-on managers with experience in the respective operations. End deliverables are dashboards demonstrating the value that is realized and is sustainable.

CONSULTING SPECTRUM

IT consulting is further segmented as IT **S**trategy consulting, IT **A**rchitecture consulting, IT **P**ortfolio management, IT **P**rocess consulting, IT **G**overnance consulting, IT **I**nfrastructure consulting, IT **O**utsourcing consulting, and IT **T**ransformation consulting. Taken together they form the consulting spectrum, the answer to a business's problems when seen through an IT prism, abbreviated as SAPPGIO-T, akin to the VIBGYOR of a rainbow. The suffix T is the resultant Transformation, the pot of gold at the end of the rainbow for the business.

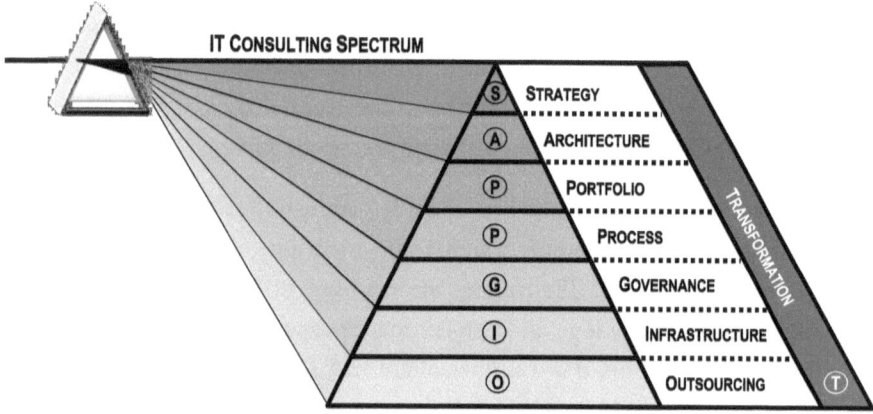

Figure 1-1: Consulting Spectrum

IT Strategy Consulting

CIOs plan strategy by analyzing the present and re-imagining the future, gauge the gaps and build strategies to bridge them, considering business needs, technology advancements, market forces, and risk appetite. CIOs need to reach out to each business unit to understand their operational strategy, aggregate their requirements for IT and produce an IT strategy, a statement expressed in business terms of the intended contribution of IT to the enterprise. Scenarios that trigger an IT strategy are – external changes in the industry, internal business change, challenges of old technology, and/or opportunities from new technologies.

IT Strategy Consulting, the 'S' in SAPPGIO-T of the IT Consulting Spectrum, primarily deals with the alignment of IT to Business and is invariably coupled with one or more of the following – IT Organization Design, Enterprise Architecture, and/or IT Infrastructure.

IT strategy therefore should be a well-thought plan of action that provides adequate guidance on how to use technology resources across the enterprise and make decisions that help bring alignment to business and achieve the corporate vision. Business Motivation Model [BMM] developed by Business Rules Group is a widely adopted industry standard for developing strategic plans.

Elements of IT Strategy

IT Vision	The stated vision of the Information Technology function, outlining the purpose of its existence, the services they provide, and most importantly, alignment to the enterprise vision. Underlying the IT vision is a set of guiding principles to translate vision into action.
IT Architecture	The design principles for understanding business from an IT perspective, primarily aimed at business process standardization and integration requirements of the organizations operating model.
IT Portfolio	The portfolio of the enterprise, prioritized programs, and projects with associated plans to monitor progress and measure performance.

IT Services	The services that the IT department delivers to the business, the agreed-upon service levels covering both business and operations.
IT Infrastructure	The underlying network and communications infrastructure that serves as a backbone for the enterprise, configurations, and capacity utilized/unutilized.
IT Governance	Governance arrangement, which includes governance mechanisms and governance processes, internally within the IT function and externally with the interfacing functions.
IT Investments	IT spending on Run the Business vs Change the Business. Comparisons with industry spending distribution on transactional vs transformational application, application development vs application maintenance.
IT Business Case	A business case is a framework for decision making, a tool to get a sense of the funding required and the expected returns, both tangible and intangible.
IT Roadmap	The minimal expected outcome of a typical IT strategy consulting engagement. A synthesis of the analysis and findings from one or more of the above elements resulting in a recommended direction to be realized incrementally.

IT strategy is developed based on a comprehensive and inter-connected study of business, technology, and organizational dimensions of the enterprise, traversing through understanding drivers, current state assessment, target state definition, analysis of gaps, evaluation of solution options, and development of recommendations based on the business case and an implementation roadmap that helps realize strategic objectives of IT and business.

IT Architecture Consulting

Architecture is foundational to any structure or system, embodied in it are the building blocks or business components, their relationships to each other, and the environment. Enterprise architecture is the bridge between strategy and planning. The primary purpose of enterprise architecture is to optimize and integrate the fragmented legacy of processes [both manual and automated] across the enterprise.

In the IT world, Enterprise Architecture [EA] provides a planning and design framework for executing IT strategy.

IT Architecture Consulting, the 'A' in SAPPGIO-T of the IT Consulting Spectrum, primarily deals with enterprise architecture definition and design. Enterprise Architecture is an integration of business, application, information, and technical architecture that helps IT become more agile to serve business requirements.

The drivers for enterprise architecture are manifold. Business drivers for EA are, when enterprises embark on business expansion, be it inorganic growth through mergers and acquisitions or organic growth through globalization or introduction of new products and services. Technically speaking, EA is mandated when enterprises are limited by legacy applications and need a technology refresh to leverage the latest technology and solutions available in the market. The Open Group Architecture Framework [TOGAF] developed by The Open Group is a vendor-neutral and technology-neutral consortium. TOGAF is a tool for assisting in the acceptance, production, use, and maintenance of architectures.

ENTERPRISE ARCHITECTURE COMPONENTS

A logical view of interactions between business components forms the blueprint for business architecture, which in turn becomes the basis for application architecture, co-relating business functions to the application portfolio. The underlying data that support the applications, including their structure and storage, shapes the information architecture. Technical architecture then is the topology of the configurations and communication protocols of all associated infrastructure elements. Individually, these architecture types are also referred to as architecture components or architecture layers. Collectively, they form the Enterprise Architecture.

1. **BUSINESS ARCHITECTURE**

   Business architecture is the basis for understanding a business from an IT perspective. It describes 'how' business is done [what processes are followed now and are expected in the future], 'who' is involved, and 'where' it is to be performed for the key business drivers to be realized.

2. **APPLICATION ARCHITECTURE**

   Application architecture is derived from business architecture. As in the case of business architecture, application components are identified from business processes, encapsulating functionality that is related, logical by principle, and manifested in software.

3. **INFORMATION ARCHITECTURE**

   Information architecture builds on the structured design of the information that serves as the means to describe, discover, access, and exchange information for fixed or recurring business transactional contexts and workflows among the parties involved. The architecture presents a holistic view of information flows in an organization including the effects of related business processes.

4. **TECHNICAL ARCHITECTURE**

   The technical architecture comprises the software and hardware capabilities required to support the deployment of business, application, and information architectures. The capabilities include IT infrastructure, middleware, networks, communications, processing, and standards.

Enterprise architecture, therefore, is a force-multiplier for organizations to achieve their business strategy. A well-defined enterprise architecture demonstrates consistency in business processes, supported by aligned applications that make available reliable and secure information over an efficient infrastructure network. Supplement this success mantra with a sound architecture governance model to make the enterprise architecture sustainable for an extended period.

IT PORTFOLIO MANAGEMENT

Portfolio Management is an essential discipline for any IT organization. Portfolio management is about helping IT get the most out of its budgets, sensitizing business constituents to the prioritization challenges that must be surmounted to ensure that the right projects get implemented, and achieving satisfactory alignment between technology spending, effort, and business goals.

IT Portfolio Management, the first 'P' in SAPPGIO-T of the IT Consulting Spectrum, primarily deals with the alignment of the application portfolio to support the business, measured in terms of functional fitment to support the business and technical maturity that is future proof, collectively enabled through the right distribution of IT investments for optimal returns.

IT Portfolio is a collection of projects aimed toward common goals. Portfolio Management, therefore, is the processes, practices, and specific activities to perform a continuous and consistent evaluation, prioritization, budgeting, and finally selection of investments that provide the greatest value and contribution to the strategic interest of the organization. In the absence of an industry-defined framework for portfolio management, most organizations have resorted to organic methods, while for investment analysis, the MIT CISR Asset Classes framework can be leveraged.

Portfolio Management Segments

The management of an IT portfolio involves simplification of business processes, rationalization of applications, consolidation and/or virtualization of infrastructure, and additionally management of IT investments.

1. **Business Process Simplification**

    Business applications are a set of software components that are visible to and recognizable by the business, they address a business need by implementing or enabling a business function. To simplify the business processes, firstly understand what the business line requires in terms of computing capability to enable the business to function. Establish a clear link between applications and the business capabilities they support. Use standard classification of business processes to effectively tag applications in the portfolio by the business capabilities they enable.

2. **Application Rationalization**

    Application rationalization is the consolidation and termination of various applications, servers, and databases. It also considers the integration of various business processes and products that are duplicated or not being utilized on account of change in demand. Application rationalization provides a framework for fact-based application life-cycle decision-making – which applications to maintain, which to invest in, which to replace and which to retire.

3. **INFRASTRUCTURE CONSOLIDATION**

Infrastructure consolidation is the optimization of the infrastructure components on which the applications that support the business run. Infrastructure includes all hardware components like servers, databases, desktops and laptops, networks, and communications. Advances in technology should be leveraged for cost reduction, increase in availability, and superior performance.

4. **INVESTMENT MANAGEMENT**

Investment management is a maturing process to evaluate, recommend and implement investments across the organization. IT investments are broadly be classified as 'Run the Business' pertaining to operational and transactional costs and 'Change the Business' the strategic costs and investments in innovation. A clear understanding of the initial distribution and ongoing performance of the same is critical to effective portfolio management.

5. **PORTFOLIO OPTIMIZATION**

Portfolio optimization is the identification of synergies from individual segments to help businesses derive greater value from their investments by making the application landscape future proof. It is about building business capability with a long term view of business and defining architecture standards to cater to this future demand. Alignment to these standards can significantly reduce application and infrastructure costs.

Finally, a unique feature to keep in mind in portfolio management engagements, unlike all other consulting engagements is that the target state is not defined upfront, but evolves as a result of the current state of the portfolio – where you are will determine how far you can or should go. This is what makes portfolio management, though assumed to be routine and simple, it is actually more complex, critical, challenging, and most importantly it needs to be continuous.

IT PROCESS CONSULTING

In the 'Technology Triad' of people, process, and technology, the process is more than just one of the three nodes, it is the glue that ties the triad together. Everyone realizes the importance of having a motivated, quality workforce, but even the finest people can't perform at their best when the process is not understood or operating at its best. IT processes determine the operational capabilities of IT, help structure the workflow within IT, and provide the ability to integrate activities, procedures, tools, technology, suppliers, people, and responsibilities.

IT Process Consulting, the second 'P' in SAPPGIO-T of the IT Consulting Spectrum, primarily deals with the definition, deployment, management, compliance, and optimization of processes and services to improve productivity and deliver resilient IT services.

Processes by definition, are a sequence of steps performed for a given purpose. In case processes are ad-hoc, descriptions not rigorously followed or enforced, highly dependent on current practitioners, such processes are termed as immature processes. Process improvement, therefore, needs to be carefully planned, executed, and sustained. The most prevalent framework in process improvement engagements is the Capability Maturity Model [CMM].

PROCESS CONSULTING DIMENSIONS

1. **PROCESS IMPROVEMENT**

   Process improvement focuses on improved availability of business-critical services through process standardization and stability, resulting in informed and timely decision making. Nature of engagements includes process benchmarking, model-based appraisals, cost of quality base-lining, and process transformation.

2. Process Optimization

Building or sustaining efficient processes is beyond the realm of process improvement or service management initiatives. Optimization and continuous improvement, efficiency, and effectiveness require lean thinking. A lean organization understands customer value and focuses its key processes to meet those needs. Lean helps to identify and eliminate wastes from these key processes.

People don't make mistakes because they want to – mistakes are made when the process allows them! Ensuring that things go right requires processes where things can't go wrong. In process consulting, improvement and optimization initiatives are continuous exercises; organizations should consider a progress appraisal once a year or two to measure the degree of improvement, the success of implementation, and impact of institutionalization.

IT Governance Consulting

The intent of IT as an organization is to ensure that it meets the business objectives and the interests of all stakeholders, the need is an institution founded on constructive leadership and collaborative structures, the ingredients to achieve compliance are processes based on a common language and a shared commitment to addressing challenges. The term that best encapsulates this inter-play is Governance.

IT Governance Consulting, the 'G' in SAPPGIO-T of the IT Consulting Spectrum, primarily deals with the entity, the IT organization. Elements critical to the successful functioning of the entity are the design of the governance structure and the definition and deployment of the governance processes.

Governance broadly comprises a structure defining responsibility and accountability, processes defining the sequence of actions to be followed, control mechanisms defining decision making, metrics to measure and monitor the performance of the organization, and a framework to facilitate the orchestration of these elements. MIT CISR has done pioneering work in this area, the Arrangement Matrix they developed is a function of what decisions are to be made and who should make the decision.

Governance Consulting Focus Areas

Governance consulting focuses on structures, the right arrangement of IT functions and their integration points with business processes highlighting the participation of business in IT matters, mechanisms to enhance business/IT alignment, and measurements to monitor performance.

1. **Governance Structures**

   Governance structures are the right arrangement of IT functions entailing how key decisions are made and who makes those decisions to align IT organization in enabling the implementation of business strategies.

2. **Governance Mechanisms**

   Governance mechanisms are roles, processes, decision-making bodies, and communication approaches that ensure effective business and IT relationships by coordinating and aligning IT to higher-level business strategies.

3. **Governance Processes**

   Governance processes are series of activities with defined responsibility and accountability and key performance indicators that specify what a business requires, to achieve its objectives and how they are fulfilled by an effective partnership between business and IT.

4. **Governance Measurements**

   Governance measurements are predefined measures encompassing lag and lead indicators linked to the IT scorecard that ensures the achievement of effective process performance. Performance metrics should be used as a basis for the formation of an IT scorecard across financial, customer, process, and learning parameters.

5. Governance Layers

The strategic layer provides direction to the functioning of IT and includes functions like strategy & planning, investment management, demand management, enterprise architecture, research & innovation, and performance management.

A tactical layer is instrumental in providing necessary support for the smooth running of IT and includes functions like application development, project management, assurance management, risk management, resource management, procurement management, vendor management, and security management.

The operations layer pertains to the day-to-day functioning of IT and includes functions like operations management, infrastructure management, application maintenance, service management, and data management.

The role of IT Governance, therefore, is to establish a structure that can maximize the value delivered by IT, through proven governance processes. The structure in turn is strengthened by well-defined roles and responsibilities. The roles mandate specific decision-making mechanisms pertinent to the specific IT domain. The mechanisms are supported by measurements that rightfully reflect their performance and are monitored by empowered committees. The beauty of this sequence is that it can withstand new business models, changing business practices, and also balance IT costs.

IT Infrastructure Consulting

Infrastructure, the very term implies a collection of physical assets assembled to provide a set of services that enable efficient operations for the enterprise. Extending this premise to the IT world, IT infrastructure would therefore be the entire computing platform; comprising hardware, software, networks, telecommunications, and the facilities that host these physical assets.

IT Infrastructure Consulting, the 'I' in SAPPGIO-T of the IT Consulting Spectrum, primarily deals with planning and design of the required infrastructure components, budget distribution for capital expenditure and operational expenditure, right-selecting components, and right-sizing configurations, operating level agreements, and opportunities for consolidation or optimization.

IT infrastructure is the critical link that provides the capability to run business applications and business processes efficiently. Key factors that impact the business from an IT infrastructure perspective are availability, performance, scalability, sustainability, and security. ITIL framework developed by Office of Government Commerce, UK, provides guidelines for service lifecycle management of IT.

INFRASTRUCTURE CONSULTING FOCUS AREAS

1. **INFRASTRUCTURE UTILIZATION**

   Infrastructure utilization refers to the percentage of capacity in use by either servers or storage or network or the data center as a whole. In infrastructure operations, higher utilization is not always the best of situations. The infrastructure must have adequate free available capacity at all times to accommodate for sudden peaks in business transactions or unplanned capacity expansion.

2. **INFRASTRUCTURE SPEND**

   Infrastructure investment or spend is the cost of infrastructure assets and infrastructure operations taken together is the single largest cost component in any firm's total IT spend. Infrastructure spend categories are hardware spend and software spend, each of which has a capital expenditure component and an operating expenditure component.

3. **INFRASTRUCTURE OPTIMIZATION**

   Optimization can be in the form of standardizing infrastructure, restructuring maintenance, rationalizing external services, adjusting end-user computing, procuring licenses based on usage, readjusting test/production environments, and future-proofing infrastructure configurations to reduce costs, increase productivity, and extend the longevity of infrastructure investments.

   Infrastructure systems should scale gracefully to support increasing volumes, if proportional processing, storage, and communication resources are made available. Infrastructure should exhibit architectural features that enhance maintainability, enable easy configurability and support 24x7 operations. Systems should be standardized on platforms that can support a diverse set of applications. Hardware, operating system, middleware, and other platforms should be consolidated across a type of delivery architecture to avoid the complexity of the environment. Security access should be enforced at the data, function, and network levels, ideally through single-sign-on.

IT Outsourcing Consulting

Outsourcing is the act of transferring some of the company's recurring internal activities and decision rights to outside providers, as set in a contract. Companies have strategically used outsourcing to improve time to market, reduce IT costs, access talent, adopt new technology, and get the flexibility of just-in-time resources. Outsourcing offers strategic and economic benefits that are far too compelling to ignore.

IT Outsourcing Consulting, the 'O' in SAPPGIO-T of the IT Consulting Spectrum, primarily deals with organizational readiness for outsourcing, outsource-ability analysis of technology components, resourcing model based on capability and capacity analysis, designing a sustainable outsourcing model, evaluating the best suited offshore locations and a mutually agreed upon service level agreement.

Outsourcing enables organizations to focus on their core business, additionally, it reduces costs, provides access to skilled resources, improves process quality, and takes advantage of differences in time zones. While outsourcing is a tool for cost-effective service, its effectiveness and whether it can be successful or not depends on how it is designed, implemented, and managed. In the absence of an industry body, there is no single framework for outsourcing. Consulting firms and service providers thus built their own frameworks based on experience and best practices.

Outsourcing Consulting Dimensions

Outsourcing models include simple staff augmentation, co-sourcing, multi-sourcing, managed services, build-operate-transfer, joint venture, shared services or captive centers, etc. Staff augmentation entails adding resources on contract, based on demand and supply. Whereas co-sourcing is working in collaboration with the service provider's resources. Multi-sourcing refers to working with a pool of preferred suppliers. In managed services model the onus of management and operations rests with the service provider. Build operate transfer refers to the scenario where the service provider builds an outsourcing center, operates it for a fixed duration, and then transfers it back to the client. Shared services or captive centers are client owned and operated service delivery centers.

1. **OUTSOURCING CONSULTING**

   The advent of outsourcing was in application outsourcing, predominantly around application maintenance later extended to application development, followed by infrastructure outsourcing and then business process outsourcing.

   Application outsourcing consulting involves an analysis of the organization's application portfolio to define a strategic roadmap based on outsource-ability analysis, cost-benefit analysis, target operating model analysis, knowledge transition plans, resourcing models, and structure of the retained organization to manage outsourcing. In business process outsourcing, the emphasis is on business areas, business functionalities, and business processes. In infrastructure outsourcing, the emphasis is on the infrastructure facilities and infrastructure services.

2. **SHARED SERVICES CONSULTING**

   Shared services are an operational model that involves centralizing common functions in one or more physical location[s] that were once performed in more or less a similar fashion by different divisions or business units of the company. As the consolidation of common functions progresses, work is standardized and redundancies minimized. Shared services boost efficiency, quality and at the same time reduce cost by leveraging economies of scale. A good starting point is establishing a shared services center for IT. The center can subsequently be expanded to support business processes in functional areas like human resources, finance, and accounting.

3. **Captive Centre Consulting**

   Companies not satisfied with savings from conventional outsourcing, constrained by dependencies on service providers set up their own captive centers, particularly prevalent in the high-tech sector, where companies may already have offshore research and development centers, and in the financial services sector where companies are looking to reduce costs and/or better secure their internal systems.

   In some sense, captive centers are an extension of shared service centers. The difference being, in the case of shared services the center can be set independently by the company or in partnership with a service provider in the company's host country or at a nearshore/offshore location, in captive centers the duality disappears, it is established by the company in an offshore location.

Post outsourcing, in addition to cost savings, organizations end up developing capabilities for improved productivity, quality, and accelerated time-to-market based on processes that focus on responsibility, accountability, measurement, reporting, and continuous improvement. The real benefit is in the resulting self-funding model for strategic initiatives.

IT Transformation Consulting

Transformation is turning vision into action, triple action to be precise – breaking from the past, managing the present, and investing in the future all in tandem. Transformation is making fundamental changes to the way business is conducted, significantly impacting people, processes, technology to gain a sustainable competitive advantage. Transformation is driven by the business, enabled by technology, and measured by business outcomes.

IT Transformation Consulting, the 'T' in SAPPGIO-T of the IT Consulting Spectrum, primarily deals with IT-enabled business transformation, starting with understanding transformation drivers leading to the right selection of segments of the spectrum, the relative positioning of the segments both in terms of priority and prominence, holistic analysis of core and corollary segments, resulting in a series of cross-functional recommendations for transformation.

IT Transformation is a comprehensive change to an IT organization, for which getting the right strategic vision is critical as execution is the hardest part of any transformation. IT Transformation, therefore, mandates executive commitment, a compelling business case, aligned business and technology, adequate risk management, structured governance, effective communication explained in a language which everyone can understand, and continuous focus on the challenges of change.

Transformation Management

In strategy consulting or governance consulting or outsourcing consulting the emphasis is only one segment of the spectrum. In transformation consulting, the emphasis shifts from a part to a sum of parts. Transformation programs are – high investment initiatives, run over long time horizons, and are successful only if the organization as a whole is ready to embrace the change. Thus, giving rise to the need for additional consulting capabilities in the domain of change management, risk management, and program management.

1. **Change Management**

   Managing change is a critical component of any major transformation and plays a key role in helping organizations successfully implement new strategies. Change management by definition is a structured process and set of tools for leading the people side of change.

   Change management at an organizational level involves engaging sponsors, creating ownership for the change process, and addressing cultural dynamics. Change management at the individual level involves people understanding what the change is and internalize why it is important, believing that the change is the right thing to do, be willing to step out of their comfort zone, and believe that they can make the change.

2. **Risk Management**

   Enterprises are exposed to a variety of internal and external factors that can potentially damage the business or deviate the business from its preset objectives, these uncertain events or conditions are called risks. Risk management is identifying, assessing, prioritizing, and mitigating such events proactively. While all risks cannot be mitigated because of lack of control or limitation of resources, risk management needs to factor in judicious allocation of enterprises resources to high impact risks

3. **PROGRAM MANAGEMENT**

A program is a group of related projects managed in a coordinated way to obtain benefits and control not available from managing them individually. Key components of program management are governance model, performance management, project management, and program management office; together they underpin a key critical success factor of delivery process excellence.

Transformation is embarking on a fundamental change to the way business is conducted. It must have a clear strategic rationale, explained in a language that everyone can understand and comprehend. The outcome of a transformation program depends on how clearly and comprehensively the transformation strategy, value, and risks have been articulated and communicated to all stakeholders. Successful transformations address the organizations, people, and capability aspects first, then the process and IT components. Transformation is a continuum; the journey is as important as the end.

CONSULTING CYCLE

In Consulting, the phases are not linear but cyclic, hence the phrase Consulting cycle. The reason it is cyclic is that engagements can cover the full life-cycle from understanding context to presenting recommendations or start in-between covering one or more phases ending in presenting recommendations.

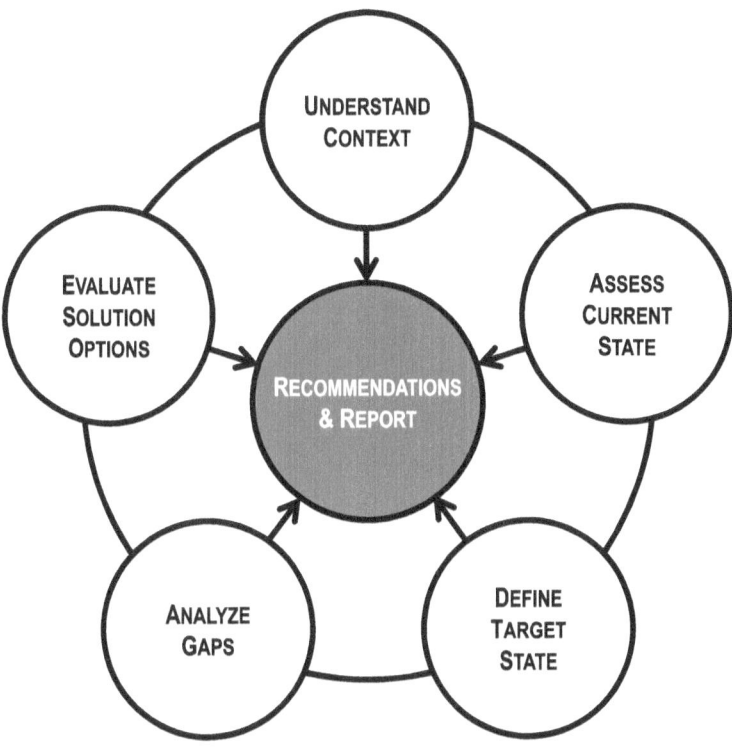

Figure 1-2: Consulting Cycle

Consulting phases or at times called consulting methodology have fancy acronyms across firms, but translated to simple English they are – a] Understanding context, b] Current state assessment, c] Target state definition, d] Gap analysis, e] Evaluating solution options, and f] Report and recommendations. The six phases are valid from an engagement model perspective, however in execution mode, in most cases, gap analysis and evaluation of solution options are merged together as analysis & findings phase. Each of these five phases is explained below, in terms of their objectives, activities, and outcomes.

A quick note on the key players to appreciate the activities better. On the client-side, there is the engagement sponsor at an executive level and reporting to him is the engagement coordinator on a full-time basis with direct ownership for engagement execution. Mirroring the same on the consultant side are the engagement partner and the engagement manager respectively.

Understanding Context

Understanding the past in terms of context and drivers is the starting point. In most Consulting engagements there is no defined problem statement, what is known at best is a certain hypothesis. The first task, therefore, is to articulate this hypothesis and arrive at a problem statement.

The objective of this phase is to understand the client context and business drivers with an open mind, putting aside past experience to uncover the specificities.

Key activities of this phase are:

1. **Synchronize with the Sponsor**

    In a one-on-one interview with the engagement sponsor, the engagement partner should walk through the context to get a better perspective of not just the cause, but also of the underlying symptoms. Determine the drivers that have necessitated the current course of action. Identify an engagement co-ordinator and prepare a list of stakeholders that need to be engaged, their profile, their span of control, and their span of responsibility. Get an understanding of the organizational culture and political dynamics.

    Explain the approach and methodology, assets, and accelerators that would be leveraged for the engagement. Introduce the engagement manager and subject matter experts that would be part of the engagement including timelines/duration of their participation. Validate schedule, milestones and confirm the deliverables, both intermediate and final. Ensure that the commercial terms and pricing schedules are understood without any ambiguity. Agree on a governance model and reporting structure.

2. **Engage with the Co-Ordinator**

    The engagement co-ordinator is identified by the engagement sponsor to represent the organization for the duration of the engagement on a full-time basis. The engagement co-ordinator along with the engagement manager from the consulting firm has complete ownership of the engagement and collective responsibility to deliver the outcomes.

Detailing of all the above activities initiated with the engagement sponsor is carried out with the engagement co-ordinator. Firstly, compile all documentation relevant to the engagement, includes corporate profile, corporate strategy, business strategy, technology strategy, reports of prior studies, etc. Schedule meetings with stakeholders in a logical sequence, share questionnaires, request for functional documentation through the co-ordinator. Similar planning is required for the subject matter experts with regard to logistics, workspace requirements, meeting schedules, etc. Jointly finalize the engagement plan, milestones, presentations, and report submission in a sufficient degree of detail.

3. **WORKSHOP WITH STAKEHOLDERS**

The engagement kick-off workshop should be called for by the engagement sponsor, facilitated by the engagement co-ordinator, participated by all stakeholders. The engagement sponsor should brief all stakeholders on the background to this initiative, spell-out scope, set expectations, request for their active participation, and introduce the engagement partner and engagement manager. The engagement co-ordinator should then elaborate on the engagement plan and seek confirmation on schedules and meetings, commitment to providing documentation, and review deliverables. The engagement manager then presents their understanding of scope, approach, methodology, and execution model, stressing the support and collaboration required to jointly realize the outcomes.

The outcome of this phase is a jointly developed and agreed upon engagement plan, detailing out the schedule, intermediate milestones, review and approval cycle, final presentation format and target audience, report structure and submission, and governance model for the course of the engagement.

CURRENT STATE ASSESSMENT

Understanding the past [context] naturally leads to assessing the present [current state] in terms of functional capability, competency of resources, and culture of the organization.

The objective of this phase is to baseline the organization and the functional areas required to be covered by the engagement.

Key activities of this phase are:

1. **REVIEW BASELINE DOCUMENTATION**

   Baseline documents have a wealth of information, what is required is revisiting the same to extract insights to address current challenges. Baseline documents consist of organizational collateral, research material, consulting artifacts, and internal reports.

   Organizational collateral includes corporate website, annual reports, and sales & marketing collateral. Browsing the corporate website helps gain insights into the organization's history, vision, and mission, growth model whether organic or inorganic and geographic spread. Annual reports provide information on the financial performance of the organization, and other useful data-points like the structure of the organization, profiles of board members, and management team; there may be a past acquaintance or a well-wisher. Sales & marketing collateral help appreciate the breadth of the product mix or the depth of services offered.

   Consulting artifacts are presentations or reports consisting of findings and/or recommendations from previous engagements. Organizations share these reports to ensure alignment to strategic directions or to validate throughput for implementation. Internal reports as the name implies are outputs of internal studies, functional documentation, business process definitions, technology landscape, and key performance indicators.

2. **INTERVIEW STAKEHOLDERS**

   Organization specific information is gathered through interviews with individual stakeholders and validated through focused workshops at a function level.

   Individual interviews are facilitated discussions leveraging customized questionnaires to gain insights into the functioning of the organization in general, their department in particular, and the challenges they face. Also, use this opportunity to hear out personal opinions and potential solutions.

Focused workshops are scheduled on a need basis to share a common viewpoint or to resolve matters of conflict, be it intra-functional or cross-functional. These workshops are facilitated by the consultants as neutral observers presenting the varied viewpoints heard, sharing similar experiences and best practices. The end objective is to create consensus.

3. **CURRENT STATE REPORT**

Current state assessment relies on information that is made available by the stakeholders, without any inferences to external data-points or any reference to the desired end state. Therefore, the analysis possible at this stage is based on preliminary observations, plotted as Heat map's or populated as a Strengths, Weaknesses, Opportunities, Threats [SWOT] analysis grid.

The outcome of this phase is a report on the current state of the organization and relevant functional areas, depicting the baseline, benchmark [where applicable], and barriers to change the status quo.

TARGET STATE DEFINITION

Having understood the past [context] and assessed the present [current state], the next logical step is defining the future [target state] in terms of the required functionality of the target environment.

The objective of this phase is to visualize the required features of the target state and validate the gaps to be bridged.

Key activities of this phase are:

1. **BIG PICTURE ENVISIONING**

The approach in the current state assessment is bottom-up, individual interview inputs aggregated at a functional level, validated through workshops and presented to engagement sponsor. However, for target state definition, the preferred approach is top-down starting with envisioning big-picture with the engagement sponsor, factoring in external data, be it the consultant's past experiences, best practices, competitive insights, critical success factors, or analyst reports.

The strategic options are then presented to the steering committee, the approving authority for an in-principle agreement on the overall direction. Members of the steering committee are the CXOs, with participation from the engagement sponsor and engagement partner.

2. Scenario Planning

Big-picture envisioning pegs the end-point; scenario planning is about exploring ways to reach this endpoint. The focus is on listing the options that are best suited for the current context. In scenario planning, external data is further leveraged to articulate realistic routes to reach the target state.

Short-listed scenarios are then presented to the management committee, the approving authority for an in-principle agreement on the validity of the scenarios. Members of the management committee are the functional heads, with participation from the engagement sponsor, engagement co-ordinator & engagement partner, and engagement manager.

3. Target State Report

Target state definition takes into account, both the internal assessment findings and external data-points to build the big-picture and list potential scenarios to realize the target state.

The big-picture highlights, the strategic direction as to how the organization as a whole would look like, including the different components describing their functions and features. Potential scenarios are strategic options available to design and develop these functions, the building blocks for the new organization.

The focus is creating a sustainable end state, which is best achieved by incremental developments of the functions, implemented in phases, resulting in an improvised organization over a time horizon.

The outcome of this phase is a report on the target state for the organization and relevant functional areas, illustrating the desired end state and scenario options that could potentially bridge the gap.

ANALYSIS & FINDINGS

The analysis & findings phase is core and critical to the success of the engagement, as the insights from these findings help shape the recommendations, the future course of action for the organization to realize its objectives.

The objective of this phase is to analyze the gaps, evaluate solution options and validate findings from the analysis.

Key activities of this phase are:

1. **ANALYZE GAPS**

   Gap analysis, as the name suggests is to identify the difference between the current state and the target state, how valid the gap is how big the gap is and how difficult the gap is to bridge.

   In analyzing the validity of the gap, what is actually being re-validated is the correctness of the current state and feasibility of the target state, necessitating a re-assessment, if needed, before evaluating solution options. Measuring how big the gap is helps in being realistic on recommendations. And assessing how difficult the gap is to bridge, allows for a rightful definition of the timelines to achieve the target state.

2. **EVALUATE SOLUTION OPTIONS**

   Solution options are evaluated for each of the feasible and prioritized gaps, in a two-step process – a standalone evaluation followed by a collective evaluation of one or more related gaps.

   In the standalone evaluation, each gap is evaluated in isolation taking into consideration the effort/resources required and the time to bridge the individual gap. In collective evaluation, the standalone solution options are evaluated on a comparative basis in terms of potential cross-impact and possible synergies of alternative or aligned solutions. A business case is prepared for the optimal solution option.

3. **VALIDATE FINDINGS**

Analysis findings are then presented to the management committee, the approving authority for an in-principle agreement on the validity of the findings, a pre-requisite to articulate recommendations. The presentation should cover – context, current state assessment findings, target state definition, gap analysis, and summary of findings with solution options. This forum is also used to discuss draft recommendations to gain general concurrence and internal buy-in.

The outcome of this phase is an interim presentation on the analysis, findings, and evaluated solution alternatives to realize the target state.

REPORT & RECOMMENDATIONS

The final phase of the consulting engagement, a culmination of all the hard work, and a moment to gain credibility.

The objective of this phase is to present recommendations and prepare the consulting report.

Key activities of this phase are:

1. **PRESENT RECOMMENDATIONS**

Recommendations are run past the engagement sponsor first and then presented to the steering committee. All recommendations should have rationale from two perspectives, an internal situation that would benefit from this recommendation and a related external best practice that the organization could learn and leverage. All recommendations should be accompanied by a business case with a clear return on investment.

2. Prepare Consulting Report

The consulting report is the final deliverable, a summary of the complete engagement proceedings.

Sample contents for the consulting report:

Chapter 1	Introduction
	Engagement context, Engagement model, Engagement plan.
Chapter 2	Current State Assessment
	Stakeholders interviewed. Summary of observations on the current state of the organization and its functions. Heat maps and SWOT analysis.
Chapter 3	Target State Definition
	Big picture vision and envisioned scenarios that would help meet the organizational objectives. Definition and description of the target state.
Chapter 4	Analysis & Findings
	Analysis of the gaps between current and target state. Findings with solutions options to bridge the gap.
Chapter 5	Recommendations on Way forward
	Recommendations with rationale and roadmap for implementation.
Appendices	Additional information on methodologies, tools, and techniques, consulting team profiles, etc.

KEY LEARNINGS

Consulting is advisory services aimed at enabling change and the creation of value for customers in the context of their business environment. The Consulting space comprises Strategy consulting, Business consulting, Functional consulting, IT consulting, and Operations consulting.

IT Consulting is further segmented into, IT Strategy consulting, IT Architecture consulting, IT Portfolio management, IT Process consulting, IT Governance consulting, IT Infrastructure consulting, IT Outsourcing consulting and IT Transformation consulting abbreviated as SAPPGIO-T and referred to as the IT Consulting spectrum,

In Consulting, the phases are not linear but cyclic, hence the phrase consulting cycle. The reason it is cyclic is that engagements can cover the full life-cycle from understanding context to the current state assessment, target state definition, analysis, and findings, leading to report and recommendations or start in-between covering one or more phases ending in presenting recommendations.

. Ω .

CHAPTER 2

'MYSTERY' OF CONSULTING

Consulting retrospective presented a classical view of consulting; while it is perfectly valid to meet the objectives of the engagement in line with the terms of reference from a practitioner's perspective. However, when seen from the end customer's perspective as in the client's organization or the extended customer [i.e.] the client's customer – the consumer's point of view, opportunities for improvements may surface, be it in the form of a problem, a process, a person or a proposition, a symptom or a solution.

In 'The Design of Business[2] Roger Martin unveils a new way of thinking – the Knowledge Funnel' balancing exploration of new knowledge [innovation] with the exploitation of current knowledge [efficiency] to regularly generate breakthroughs and create value for companies.

In this chapter, the 'Mystery' of Consulting, the thinking behind the knowledge funnel is articulated and applied to consulting to explore the mysteries of consulting, that can be extrapolated further leveraging Design Thinking.

THE KNOWLEDGE FUNNEL

Knowledge Funnel is a three-stage process, the graphic model below shows how knowledge proceeds through the funnel. The first stage of the funnel is the exploration of a mystery, which takes an infinite variety of forms. The next stage of the funnel is a heuristic, a rule of thumb that helps narrow the field of inquiry and work the mystery down to a manageable size. As an organization puts its heuristic into operation, studies it more, and thinks about it intensely that it can

---

2 Martin, R. (2009), *The Design of Business,* Harvard Business Press.

convert a general rule of thumb to fixed formulae; formulae is an algorithm the last stage of the knowledge funnel.

Design Thinking focuses on accelerating the pace at which knowledge advances from mystery to heuristic to algorithm. Initially, design thinkers have to look at everything as they don't yet know what to leave. Mysteries are expensive, time-consuming, and risky, they are worth tackling only because of the potential benefits of discovering a path out of the mystery to the revenue-generating heuristic.

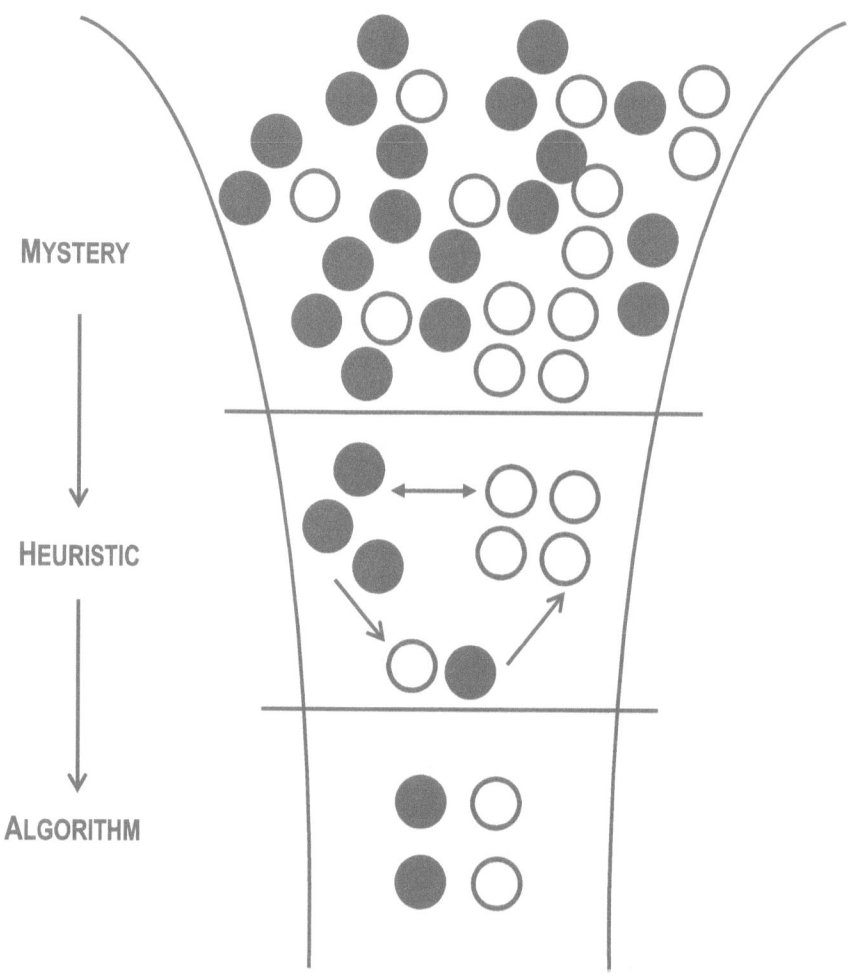

Figure 2-1: Knowledge Funnel

Mysteries of Consulting

Knowledge funnel for design thinking in consulting starts with mysteries, which can occur in any of the consulting phases and for any of the consulting segments. Mysteries of consulting are – mystery of hypothesis, stakeholders, assumptions, interviews, current state, target state, analysis and recommendations as explained below:

1. **Mystery of Hypothesis**

   In consulting, as articulated earlier the problem statement is derived from a problem hypothesis, which in itself is an abstract synthesis of the sponsor's and/or key stakeholder's viewpoint, seldom that of the end customer or the extended customer. Despite this ambiguity, the stated hypothesis becomes the gospel truth in defining the objective and outcome of the engagement. Furthermore, hypothesis as a technique relies heavily on experience and expertise, in this case, that of the consultant and the client and not the real consumer. The mystery lies in the fact that any error in the hypothesis would have a ripple effect all through the engagement.

2. **Mystery of Stakeholder's**

   In consulting, the consultant's interactions are predominantly at the executive level for almost everything, from understanding the context to drivers for change, challenges to the business, competitive landscape, contemplating the future, and for crafting transformational initiatives that would address the objectives and deliver upon the outcomes, which are perfectly valid from a strategic dimension. The mystery lies in the fact that there is limited emphasis on the operational dimension, insights for which are best gained from, where else, but from the ground-staff.

3. **Mystery of Assumptions**

   In consulting, given the short duration of the engagement, several assumptions are made throughout the course of the engagement, be it in building the hypothesis, analyzing the cause or effect, or articulating recommendations.

While assumptions are required, the critical factor is their degree of accuracy and how they are contained. The mystery lies in the fact that assumptions made are valid at a certain point in time, the underlying facts and figures are, however, open to scrutiny over a period of time.

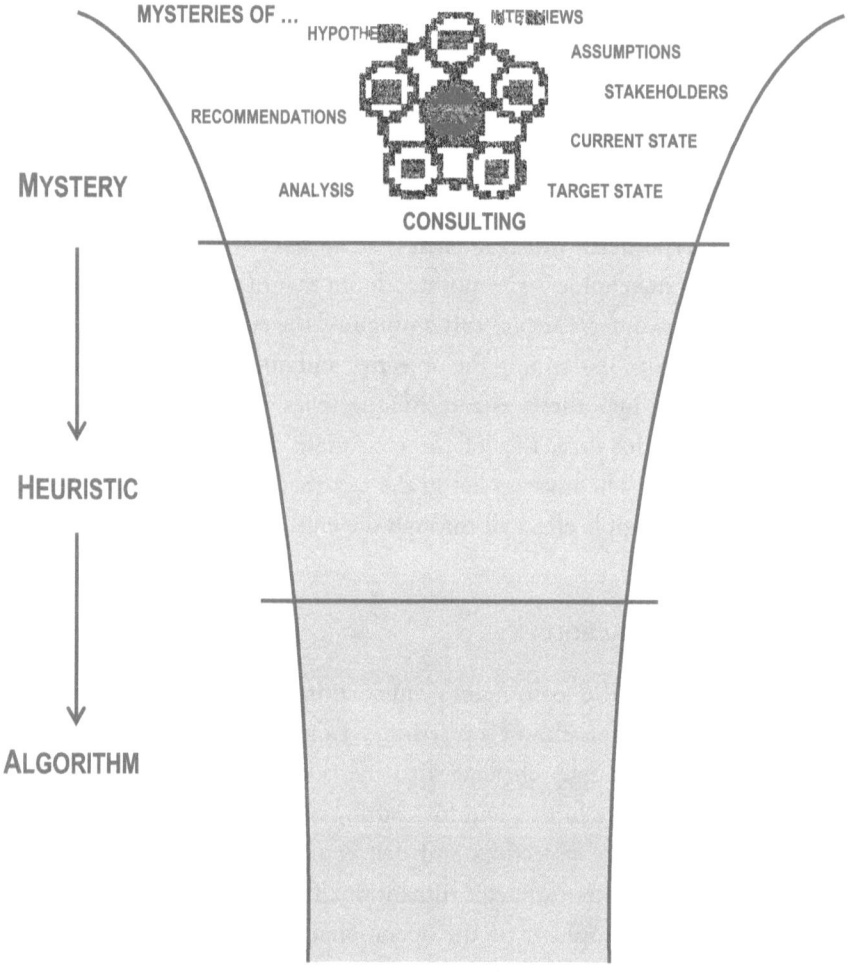

Figure 2-2: Mysteries of Consulting

4. Mystery of Interviews

In consulting, the primary mode of information gathering is through interviews by the consultant with key executives pre-dominantly based on pre-defined questionnaires. Even in the case of workshops, the modus operandi is still the same; the proceedings continue to be driven by the consultant using pre-defined agendas from the firm's knowledge repository. The mystery lies in the fact that there is limited attempt to enquire using open-ended questions.

5. Mystery of Current State

In consulting, the context is invariably assessed on internal factors like the firm's current situation and/or capability, ignoring the fact that the real drivers for change are a reaction to external factors like regulatory compliance, share in existing markets, and growth in emerging markets, margin management or operational efficiency. Remember, consultants are called-in only when one or more of these parameters are not as desired on the dashboard. The mystery lies in the fact that there is an inherent tendency to assume that something is broken internally either in existing processes or capabilities.

6. Mystery of Target State

In consulting, the target state is defined by the various corrections required to the current state. Like in the case of context, corrections are also arrived at considering the opposite of what is really required. Corrections are invariably addressed taking into account external factors like industry trends, market dynamics, geography specifics, and competitor play, ignoring the fact that the real correction can be sustainable only when it comes from within considering the organizational culture and capability. The mystery lies in the fact that there is an inherent tendency to assume that something that worked well for others will work for all and yield the same results.

7. Mystery of Analysis

In consulting, analysis is based on benchmarking internal data with industry trends which are dynamic and influenced by numerous factors like sponsors of survey, sources of data, and size of a sample. The mystery lies in the fact that benchmarks by themselves are not foolproof either, in the sense that a deviation from average while healthy for one firm may prove to be detrimental for another firm.

8. **Mystery of Recommendations**

In consulting, every observation or finding goes through several stages of evaluation to determine its potential to create positive business value before it becomes an actionable recommendation. The mystery lies in the fact that what appears to be a quick win based on current context and analysis, may turn out to be an implementation nightmare.

Key Learnings

Consulting when seen from the end customer's perspective as in the client's organization or the extended customer [i.e.] the client's customer – the consumer's point of view, opportunities for improvements may surface, be it in the form of a problem, a process, a person or a proposition, a symptom or a solution.

The three stages of Roger Martin's Knowledge funnel are – Mystery [an exploration], Heuristic [a rule of thumb], and Algorithm [converting a rule of thumb to fixed formulae]. Design Thinking focuses on accelerating the pace at which knowledge advances from mystery to heuristic to algorithm.

Mystery in the context of Consulting is, how best to bring in a human-centered approach to enrich experiences of end customers and extended customers and to sustain consulting solutions over a period of time.

. Ω .

Part Two
Design Thinking

Chapter 3

Design Thinking Perspective

Traditionally, the word 'Design' is used to describe the visual aesthetics of the objects. However, the meaning of this word has evolved, and it is not that limited anymore. Nowadays, design is not just about form or physical attributes; it is about a new method of thinking. This method refers to the development of products and services, putting customers' needs at the heart of the development strategy, and using creative and innovative techniques, collectively articulated as 'Design Thinking'.

Design thinking identifies and investigates known and ambiguous aspects of the current situation to discover hidden parameters and open alternative paths that may lead to the goal. Because design thinking is iterative, intermediate "solutions" are also potential starting points of alternative paths, including redefining the initial problem, in a process of co-evolution of problem and solution.

Design thinking employs divergent thinking as a way to ensure that many possible solutions are explored in the first instance, and then convergent thinking as a way to narrow these down to a final solution. Divergent thinking is the ability to offer different, unique, or variant ideas adherent to one theme while convergent thinking is the ability to find the correct solution to the given problem. Design thinking encourages divergent thinking to ideate many solutions [possible or impossible] and then uses convergent thinking to prefer and realize the best resolution.

The objective of the method is not for business people to become actual designers, but rather to build on the belief that much can be learned from a designer's way of working and thinking to spark creativity and effectively address complex business issues.

In this chapter, the Design Thinking Evolution, Understanding Design Thinking from definitions to elements, attributes, application to business, the culture of design thinking and its future, plus overviews of Design Thinking Frameworks are presented to provide a full perspective of Design Thinking.

Design Thinking Evolution

In 60's America, professions like industrial design and product design made their first small steps to distance themselves from engineering and the sciences. However, they did not get very far, industrial design was still mostly based on quantifiable facts, things that could be proven, measured, and improved upon, designer's workplace was still in a university laboratory or on a factory floor.

Subjects like ergonomics and design science determined design decisions, demonstrating that designers had highly specialized ways of working. Design Science as an example was spearheaded by all-round inventor Buckminster Fuller at MIT in the mid-fifties. Rare for that period, Fuller created design teams comprised of experts from across disciplines to tackle systemic failures.

In his own words, Fuller called Design Science, "The effective application of the principles of science to the conscious design of our total environment in order to help make the earth's finite resources meet the needs of all humanity without disrupting the ecological processes of the planet". He created systematic methods to evaluate, design, and solve problems. His goals were grand. He wanted to use the potential of science and technology to intentionally advance the well-being and standard of living of everyone. What he did in the 50's and 60's resonates with the design thinking of today because his teams were not designers but people who were expert enough in their fields to contribute to the goal of a project. In Fuller's approach success was measured so that projects were replicable.

The concept of design thinking was developed by social scientist and Nobel laureate Herbert A. Simon in his book 'The Sciences of the Artificial' in 1969. Simon argued that "Everything designed should be seen as artificial as opposed to natural. The engineer, and more generally the designer should be concerned with how things ought to be in order to attain goals and how to function".

In 60's Europe, around the same time as an absolute counter to Fuller, Scandinavian participatory design or cooperative design was also getting off the ground. Unlike the teams of experts assembling in America to fix the world, the Scandinavians invited everyone to become involved in discussions on design; here designers played the role of facilitators or guides, with everyone from experts to workers and inhabitants co-designing products and services they would want to use.

The cooperative design was grounded on the belief that every worker "has the right and duty to participate in decisions concerning" what systems are developed and how those systems are designed. On the flip side, the disadvantage of the participative design was its negligence towards user experience and stakeholder input.

Donald Norman a design theorist redefined participatory design into what he coined as 'User-Centered Design'. User testing became less about usability and more about a user's interests and needs. Another significant shift in ideology was the placement of the user at the center of the development process, emphasizing experience over efficiency and adopted a more humanistic approach with the involvement of the user throughout the development of a product or system.

Subsequently, a new perspective started to emerge in business, understanding how and what the user does with a product [or service] including their journey and experience – another step forward in the evolution of design methodology, attention shifted to understanding the use, interaction, and journey of that product/service after it has left the hands of the provider.

Furthermore, service design extended the definition of the user to include all stakeholders and individuals affected or interacting with the service system, this way of working relied heavily on designers – designing-by-doing, mock-up environment, future circles, organizational games, co-operative prototyping, ethnographic field research, and democratic dialogue to generate new ideas or improve on existing ones.

Highly involved and iterative, this mode of presenting and working through designs acted as provocations or discussion starters between all the workshop participants. Not limited to creating physical artifacts, often this approach has seen designer/facilitators co-creating new systems, services, and even policies with the people who will in the end be using them daily.

The human-centered design evolved in the late 1990s when the development of methods described above shifted from a technology-driven focus to a humanized one. The holistic perspective introduced in service design allowed the human-centered design to transform from a method to a mindset aiming to humanize the design process and empathize with stakeholders.

Nigel Cross was a researcher in the field of human-computer interaction before he began investigating design methodology. His seminal book 'Designerly Ways of Knowing' looks at what makes the way designers think and make decisions different from other professions a great influence which helped in the construction of design thinking. To Nigel, "Everyone can and does design. We all design when we plan for something new to happen, whether that might be a new version of a recipe, a new arrangement of the living room furniture, or a new lay tour of a personal web page. Design thinking is something inherent within human cognition; it is a key part of what makes us human".

Design thinking, as a method of creative action and innovation, was considerably expanded by Rolf Faste at Stanford University in the 1980s and 1990s. In the business context, design thinking was adapted by Faste's Stanford colleague David Kelley who started a new program where students from different backgrounds could nurture their creative talents and apply their newfound skills to tough challenges. The institute came to be known as 'd-school', officially as 'Hasso Plattner Institute of Design' thanks to funding from Plattner the founder of SAP.[3]

David Kelley is also the founder of IDEO – a firm that pioneered the contemporary and current view of design thinking. Tim Brown, an Industrial Designer, and IDEO's CEO has been a great advocate for design thinking and innovation, promoting design thinking for non-designers. In order to survive in today's complex world, organizations need to generate, embrace, and execute new ideas, which take creativity and a creatively capable workforce. It's the secret

---

3   Kelley, D. & Kelley, T. (2013), *Creative Confidence*, William Collins.

sauce, or in evolutionary terms, it's what keeps you fit. Organizations without it can't compete.

IDEO's innovation process, from creating hot teams to learning to see through the customer's eyes and brainstorming and rapid prototyping are primetime lessons in creativity, spread to the world at large by Tom Kelley, best-selling author, leading innovation speaker, partner at IDEO, and brother of David Kelley through his international bestsellers 'The Art of Innovation' and 'The Ten Faces of Innovation'.[4,5] Innovation is about seeing the world, not as it is, but as it could be. It's about exploring really 'wicked problems' whose solutions can't be found in past experiences or proven by data.[6]

Understanding Design Thinking

Design thinking is a strong advocate of problem-solving based on first principles. What better way to understand design thinking than by exploring the first principles of design thinking itself, starting with definitions, elements and moving onto the business of design thinking, characteristics that are mutually exclusive but collectively exhaustive.

Design Thinking Definitions

The concept of 'intuition' is a convenient shorthand word for design thinking, in its simplest form, it means thinking as a designer would!

According to Tim Brown, CEO IDEO, "Design Thinking is a discipline that uses the designer's sensibility and methods to match people's needs with what is technologically feasible and what a viable business strategy can convert into customer value and market opportunity".[7]

Design thinking is an approach to innovation that is powerful, effective, and broadly accessible, that can be integrated into all aspects of business and society. And that individuals and teams can use to generate breakthrough ideas that are implemented and that therefore have an impact.

---

4   Kelley, T. (2016), *The Art of Innovation*, Profile Books.
5   Kelley, T. (2016), *The Ten Faces of Innovation*, Profile Books.
6   Martin, R. (2009), *The Design of Business*, Harvard Business Press.
7   Martin, R. (2009), *The Design of Business*, Harvard Business Press.

Design thinking, fundamentally, recognizes that design should achieve the purpose and business goals, not just beauty. Design thinking shifts the focus from a business-centric engineering solution [we invent a product based on a bunch of assumptions and cross our fingers that it will work for customers] to a customer-centric solution [we explore cultural phenomena, observe how people behave and think, gain insights into what they need, and design a product around that]. Design thinking, therefore, solves problems and redesigns tasks by working from the viewpoint of the user to come up with a new approach to processes that address common pain points.

Design researcher Alistair Fuad-Luke synthesizes the various definitions of Design Thinking succinctly as follows – The real 'Joy' of design is to deliver fresh perspectives, improved well-being, and an intuitive sense of balance with the wider world. The real 'Spirit' of design elicits some higher meaning. The real 'Power' of design is that professionals and laypeople can co-design in amazingly creative ways. The real 'Beauty' of design is its potential for secular, pluralistic expression. The real 'Strength' of design is this healthy variance of expression. The real 'Relevance' of design is its ability to be proactive. The real 'Passion' of design is in its philosophical, ethical and practical debate".

DESIGN THINKING ELEMENTS

Design thinking integrates what is desirable from a human point of view with what is technologically feasible and economically viable. Design thinking relies on our ability to be intuitive, recognize patterns and construct ideas that have emotional meaning and functionality. Design thinking is a way of describing a set of principles that are applied by diverse people to a wide range of problems.[8]

Reinforcing elements of successful design are:

- **INSIGHT**

    Design thinking is a creative journey and insights are the heart and soul of design thinking. Traditional methods of data analysis may help uncover certain perspectives but insights reveal the unobvious and untold aspects.

---

8   Brown, T. (2009), *Change by Design*, Harper Collis.

Insights help understand relations between products and users as well as between users and users.

- **OBSERVATION**

    The best insights are revealed when we observe the users in an unrestricted and free environment where they work, live, and spend their time. Watching people perform their work helps us understand what they don't do and why, what they don't say and why.

- **EMPATHY**

    Empathizing is one of the best ways to connect with the target audience whom we are observing. In other words, standing in their shoes who we want to know more about. This is the fundamental difference between the traditional approach and design thinking. Instead of validating assumptions or test an approach, design thinking is about creating powerful insights from observations and later creating products and services that really improve lives.

DESIGN THINKING IN BUSINESS

The business world is a reliability-oriented place, the bulk of the organization, therefore, would be reliability-driven design thinkers. But the organization also needs validity driven people to keep the organization from stagnating through overexploitation and under exploration. There are five things that design thinkers must do to be more effective at the extreme of the reliability and validity spectrum.[9]

1. **REFRAME EXTREME VIEWS AS A CREATIVE CHALLENGE**

    Design thinking welcomes extreme views, something which can be truly out of the box. At first extreme views may seem impossible, but they often lead to a truly creative and game-changing opportunity. However, to gain broader acceptance, the design thinker has to tactfully balance such extreme views and associated opportunities. Design thinkers should find ways to

---

9   Martin, R. (2009), *The Design of Business,* Harvard Business Press.

demonstrate incremental value as well as build some discipline into how to deal with extreme views.

2. **EMPATHIZE WITH YOUR COLLEAGUES AT THE EXTREMES**

   Genuinely understanding the user's perspective is the best way to design a compelling solution. It's no different for extreme views or extreme users. Effective design thinkers strive to get a deep understanding of the user's position in order to reveal the most potent options for a compelling solution. Design thinkers can gain the right insights by empathizing with the users and really understanding the way they think. The insights from users can help address the organizational needs, as well as help, embark on the best possible solution.

3. **LEARN TO SPEAK THE LANGUAGE OF BOTH RELIABILITY AND VALIDITY**

   Design thinkers need to deal with both analytical thinkers and intuitive thinkers. Analytical thinkers focus on reliability as they think about the production of consistent and predictable outcomes. Whereas intuitive thinkers focus on validity as they rely on outcomes that delight rather than outcomes that are consistent and predictable.

4. **PUT UNFAMILIAR CONCEPTS IN FAMILIAR TERMS**

   Analytical thinkers tend to make decisions based on past events whereas intuitive thinkers care more about future events. To have fruitful conversations, both analytical and intuitive thinkers need to be brought on to the same page. This is a typical challenge for design thinkers. To help analytical thinkers, the best tool for design thinkers is to craft stories that help draw analogies and demonstrate how an existing idea resembles a future idea. To help intuitive thinkers the best tool for design thinkers is to share data and reasoning rather than conclusions.

Design Thinking Perspective

5. **WHEN IT COMES TO PROOF, USE SIZE TO YOUR ADVANTAGE**

    Analytical thinkers put a lot of emphasis on proof which is substantiated based on past events, but intuitive thinkers don't care much about proof of that sort. Intuitive thinkers on the other hand can't prove in advance that their ideas will work. When dealing with intuitive thinkers, design thinkers need to slice the solution in such a way that it can demonstrate the power of innovation.

DESIGN THINKING FRAMEWORKS

Design methods are techniques, rules, or ways of doing things that someone uses within a design discipline. The Design Thinking process is best thought of as a system of overlapping spaces rather than a sequence of orderly steps. Design Thinking as a method is empirical in the sense that it is both experimental and experiential, thus giving rise to several frameworks for Design Thinking, one such framework is Roger Martin's 'Knowledge Funnel' as explained in chapter one. Few more frameworks are outlined below, only to serve as a point of reference.

d-SCHOOL FRAMEWORK

In order to fully appreciate the Stanford d-School's Design Thinking Framework[10], first, take a peek into the d-School mindsets.

- Show don't tell – Communicating vision in an impactful and meaningful way by creating experiences, using illustrative visuals, and telling good stories.

- Focus on human values – Empathy for the people you are designing for and feedback from these users is fundamental to good design.

- Craft clarity – Produce a coherent vision out of messy problems. Frame it in a way to inspire others and to fuel ideation.

- Embrace experimentation – Prototyping is not simply a way to validate an idea; it is an integral part of the innovation process.

---

10 Stanford d.School, *Design Thinking bootcamp bootleg.*

- Be mindful of the process – Know where you are in the design process, what methods to use in that stage, and what your goals are.

- Bias toward action – Design thinking is a misnomer; it is more about doing than thinking. Bias toward doing and making over thinking and meeting.

- Radical collaboration – Bring together innovators with varied backgrounds and viewpoints. Enable breakthrough insights and solutions to emerge from the diversity.

The d-School framework comprises five modes – Empathize, Define, Ideate, Prototype, and Test.

1. Empathize

Human-centric designing is based on empathy. Understanding who we are designing for and what is important to them is a pre-requisite for meaningful design. Empathizing with users helps to understand and appreciate the fundamental needs and underlying motivations of the users for whom we are designing.

Observing, Engaging, and Immersing are common ways to build strong empathy. Observing entails watching carefully what users do and don't do, how they interact with the environment. Engaging is interacting directly with the users which helps reveal about their way of thinking, values which in turn helps create meaningful insights. Last but not the least, immersing is putting ourselves into the user's shoes, this helps empathize with users and provides the first-hand experience of the user's perspective.

2. Define

Define mode is about summarizing outcomes from empathize stage into meaningful user requirements and scope a problem statement to be solved. There are two clear goals of define mode – first to develop a thorough understanding of users and second to outline an actionable problem statement, which is also called "Point of View" or PoV. The PoV clearly defines the problem to be solved using design thinking and provides the basis for evaluating solutions. In the define stage, the design team captures compelling ideas and elaborates features that will allow them to solve the problem.

3. **IDEATE**

The design team then begins to generate compelling ideas and radical solution options. By now, the design team has empathized with the user and has created a comprehensive PoV. The goal of the ideate stage is to explore various solution options that help address crucial user requirements. In this stage, the design team thinks creatively and outside the box to come up with meaningful solution options. The focus here is to generate as many as possible unique ideas. These ideas are then utilized to build prototypes of the solution.

4. **PROTOTYPE**

Prototyping is about taking the ideas into the real world. Promising ideas selected in the ideate stage are considered for prototyping. Prototypes are inexpensive, demonstrable versions of the product or features within the product. A prototype can take any form, for instance, a post-it note or a rough sketch or models built by Lego building blocks.

Prototypes are a very powerful means to bring the user close to the final product by giving it a real-life feel. Prototypes are taken to the end-users who review the prototype and highlight its shortcomings if any. Prototyping is done in iterations and each iteration brings some improvements over the previous. In addition, if the prototype fails it fails early, making the entire process inexpensive.

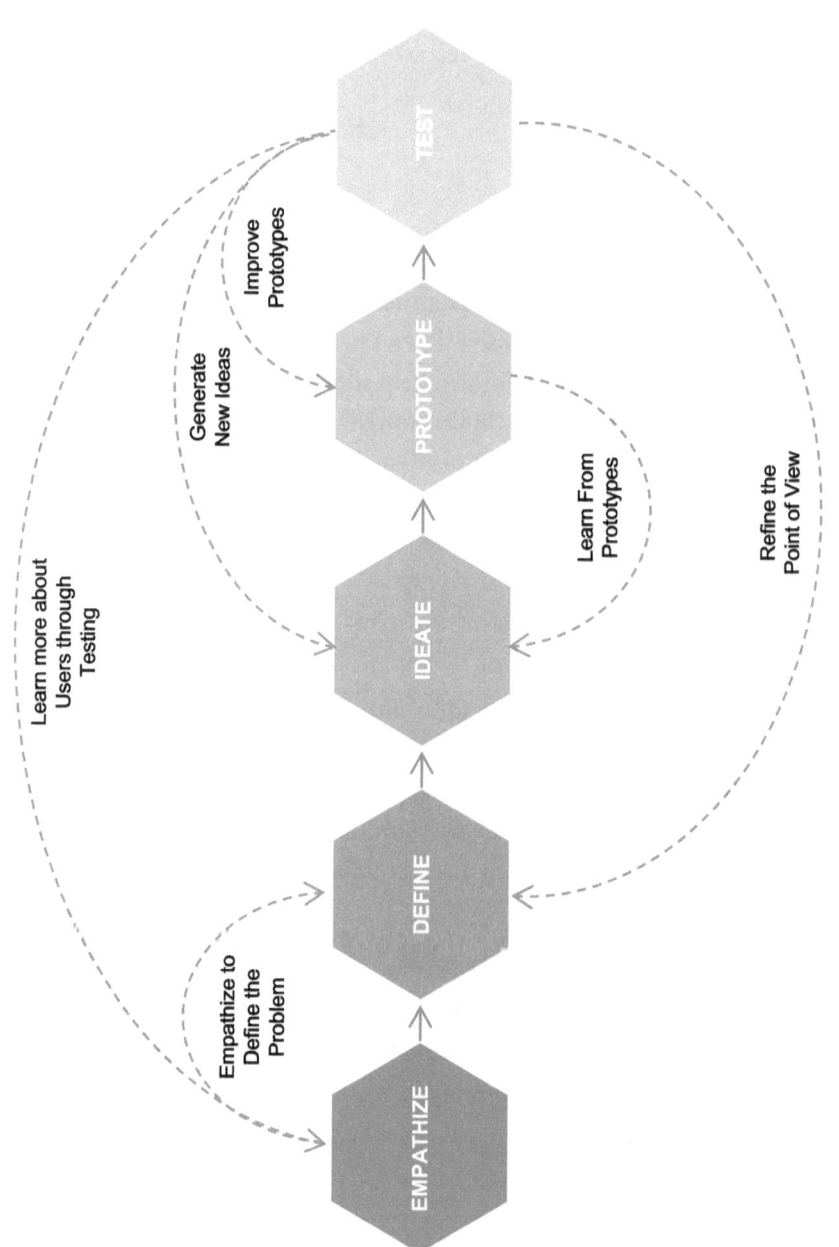

Figure 3-1: d-School Framework

5. Test

The testing stage is when the product/solution is taken directly to the end-users for evaluation in order to obtain feedback and make improvements. Testing is yet another opportunity to learn more about the users and empathize with them. Testing is conducted iteratively and deeply influences all stages of the design thinking journey. Testing is an open validation of how well we have understood the user needs. Testing provides a new set of insights into the next iteration of prototypes. Testing results provide an opportunity to re-empathize with the users, ideate more effectively and improve our PoV.

Design Thinking stages are seldom sequential. The design thinking process is carried out in a flexible and non-linear fashion. Different groups within the design team may conduct one or more stages of the process concurrently or one or more stages can be extended as required. Results from the testing phase may reveal some insights about users, which in turn may lead to another Ideate iteration or the development of new prototypes. In essence, Design Thinking is iterative, flexible, and focused on active collaboration between designers and users.

IDEO's Framework

Embracing Human-Centered Design means believing that all problems even the seemingly intractable ones are solvable; the people who face the problems every day are the ones who hold the key to the solution. Being a human-centered designer is about believing that as long as you stay grounded in what you have learned from the people, your team can arrive at new solutions that the world needs.[11]

IDEO's philosophy of design and its seven mindsets are:

1. Creative Confidence

Creativity is not restricted just to 'creative types' but anyone and everyone can be creative. 'Creative confidence' is the belief that creativity is the ability

---

11 IDEO.org (2015), *Design Kit: The Field Guide to Human-Centered Design.*

to imagine or perceive something in a new way and it can come from any corner of the organization. Creative confidence helps to develop new ideas, make them real, test them out, and learn from them. Creative confidence inspires to innovate and achieve.

2. **MAKING**

When the goal is to build impactful solutions that really work, designers can't wait to see something tangible. Making something real is a proven way to evaluate an idea and to ascertain the feasibility of a design. Making something real helps convey an idea, share it, learn from it and improve the same.

3. **LEARN FROM FAILURE**

Failures are an integral part of the design thinking journey. Experimental designs fail multiple times before even coming close to an acceptable level. Each failure teaches something new and becomes the foundation of the next improvement. Designers would need the right mindset to deal with failures and learn from them.

4. **EMPATHY**

Empathy is the ability to step into someone's shoes and live their feelings to extract their perspective. Immersing yourself in someone's environment and way of working gives the opportunity to create new possibilities and discard pre-conceived notions and traditional ways of thinking.

5. **EMBRACING AMBIGUITY**

Design thinking is a way of innovating with creativity and it encourages ambiguity, curiosity, and uncertainty. Design thinking welcomes ambiguity with an open mind. Being open to ambiguity provides an opportunity to benefit from diverse thoughts and pursue solution options that were earlier difficult to imagine.

6. OPTIMISM

Optimism is the thread that ties together all stages of the design thinking process. Optimism is to embrace the possibility that an idea can work even if it's in a very nascent stage. Optimism ensures persistant focus throughout the design-thinking journey and encourages to overcome countless obstacles that come along the way.

7. ITERATION

Design thinkers adopt an iterative approach to problem-solving as it helps incorporate feedback from users into the design process. Being iterative helps keep the design thinking process nimble and adaptive to feedback from users until the right idea is identified. Once the right idea is identified then the focus is to arrive at the next level of detail.

The three stages of IDEO's process are – Inspiration, Ideation, and Implementation.

1. INSPIRATION

The Inspiration stage is the very first step towards the creation of a solution. Inspiration is the problem or the opportunity, which motivates the search for a winning solution. Inspiration is about keeping people at the center of the solution, observing things in the real world, interacting with a variety of people, and understanding the motivations of people for whom we are designing a solution.

The Inspiration phase helps us better understand our target audience, their pain points, and aspirations, which becomes the foundation of the design thinking process.

2. IDEATION

The Ideation stage is about sharing with the stakeholders what we have learned about the users, and identify potential opportunities for designing a winning solution. This is the stage where lots of ideas are being generated which leads to a promising solution. These ideas are carefully scrutinized without any prejudice and the selected few ideas are put forth for prototyping. Prototypes are then shared with real users to get their feedback and learn more. This process is iterated until the right idea that has the potential to build a meaningful solution is identified.

3. **IMPLEMENTATION**

The Implementation stage will help you answer – How do I plan for what's next? How do I make my concept real? How do I assess if my solution is working?

In the implementation stage, the solution is brought to life. This is the stage where stakeholders whole-heartedly embrace the solution and realize the benefits of the solution. Solutions developed using design thinking are more likely to succeed because all concerned stakeholders have been a part of the solution.

Design Thinking Perspective 69

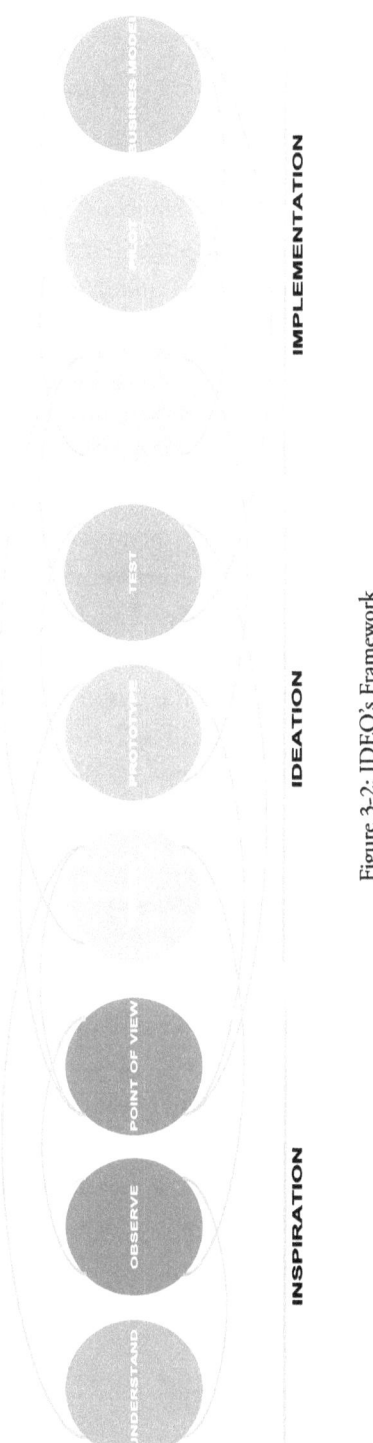

Figure 3-2: IDEO's Framework

Google's Design Sprints

Design Sprint is a framework for answering critical business questions through design, prototyping, and testing ideas with users. The core intent of this framework is to launch a product or new features and iterate it later rather than take a lot of unnecessary time to perfect it before the launch. Phases of the design sprint are – Understand, Sketch, Decide, Prototype, and Validate. Design Sprint's leverage the framework for divergent and convergent thinking as shown below:[12]

1. ### Understand

    Understand phase is about discovering the innovation opportunity, potential users, competition, business value, and measures of success. In this phase, a knowledge base is created around the innovation opportunity and shared across all stakeholders involved. Several proven design thinking tools such as 'How Might We', user interviews, and empathy-building exercises are used extensively in this phase to build the knowledge base. Stakeholders and subject matter experts across the business are invited to articulate the problem or opportunity from business, technical, competitor, and users' perspectives. This phase also lists the constraints that the design team has to work through.

2. ### Sketch

    The Sketch phase is about generating the best ideas and sketching potential solutions. In this phase, each member of the design team selects his/her best idea and sketches it out highlighting multiple states of the idea. Depending on the context, members of the design team are required to create a certain minimum number of ideas to select the most promising ones. Once the most promising ideas are identified, the next step is to storyboard the idea. Based on the best ideas, potential solutions are sketched end to end with as many details as possible.

---

12 Google, *Design Sprint Framework*.

3. DECIDE

In this phase, the design team decides which solutions are worthy enough to be taken forward. Each potential solution is put on a wall like an art gallery. There are several techniques such as voting, feasibility assessment, pros & cons, etc. that are used to select the most promising solution from the list of potential solutions. If for some reason, the design team is unable to pick the best solution then the top two best solutions are picked and taken forward.

Once the best potential solutions are identified, a common understanding is established of what the prototypes should look like and what should be the measure of success for each prototype.

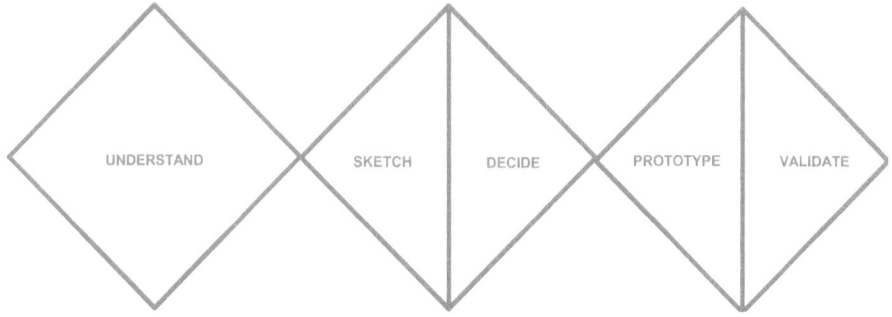

Figure 3-3: Google's Design Sprint

4. PROTOTYPE

The prototype phase is all about building the product as realistic as possible and testing it with the end-user. Based on the nature of the design problem, there are several ways of prototyping from on-screen presentations, to role-playing and 3D printing. Each prototype is built as meticulously as possible and tested several times before taking it to the end-user for critique, collecting feedback, and identifying areas of improvement.

5. Validate

This phase is about validating the prototypes with a larger audience. In this phase each interaction with the end-user is observed carefully with an open mind, it provides a great learning opportunity about end-users, their level of acceptance of the solution, and areas of improvement. The prototype/solution may get rejected as well, in such cases, this method may be repeated with a different user segment or a part of the method repeated with the same user segment.

Key Learnings

Hypothesis building and scenario creation are common consulting techniques that make several viable alternatives of a future situation based on current parameters. Selecting a hypothesis and rejecting another or selecting a scenario and rejecting another is a critical activity that forms the basis of the consultant's recommendations. Design Thinking can open up new ways to make such decisions. In Design Thinking, the premise is that every idea is a good idea, irrespective of the source of the idea. Design Thinking recommends a human-centered approach to problem-solving by reaching out to all, the belief is that solutions thus built will not only be successful but also sustainable.

In the 1960s, the concept of design thinking was developed by social scientist and Nobel laureate Herbert A. Simon, who argued that "Everything designed should be seen as artificial as opposed to natural. The engineer, and more generally the designer should be concerned with how things ought to be in order to attain goals and how to function". The human-centered design evolved in the late 1990s when the development of methods described above shifted from a technology driven focus to a humanized one. The holistic perspective introduced in service design allowed the human-centered design to transform from a method to a mindset aiming to humanize the design process and empathize with stakeholders.

Design thinking, as a method of creative action and innovation, was considerably expanded by Rolf Faste at Stanford University in the 1980s and 1990s. In the business context, design thinking was adapted by Faste's Stanford colleague David Kelley is also the founder of IDEO – a firm that pioneered the contemporary and current view of design thinking. According to Tim Brown, CEO IDEO, "Design Thinking is a discipline that uses the designer's sensibility and methods to match people's needs with what is technologically feasible and what a viable business strategy can convert into customer value and market opportunity".

Design Thinking Frameworks include Roger Martin's Knowledge Funnel, Stanford's d-School Framework, IDEOs Framework, and Google's Design Sprints.

. Ω .

CHAPTER 4

'HEURISTIC' OF DESIGN THINKING

Heuristics guide us toward a solution by way of organized exploration of the possibilities. Heuristics are open-ended prompts to think or act in a particular way. Heuristics offer no guarantee that using them produces a certain result. Rather they contain the vague promise that all things being equal, using the heuristic in the context it is meant for, may on average be better for you than not using it. Heuristics represent an incomplete yet distinctly advanced understanding of what was previously a mystery.

In order to create value across the knowledge funnel, organizations require two very different activities, moving across the knowledge stages of the funnel from mystery to heuristic and from heuristic to algorithm and operating within each knowledge stage of the funnel by honing and refining an existing heuristic or algorithm. Organizations may engage in 'Exploration' the search for new knowledge or 'Exploitation' the maximization of payoff from existing knowledge.[13] [2] The key is to maintain a balance as both activities create value, and both are critical to the success of any organization.

In this chapter, the mysteries of consulting are revisited to find a pattern. Patterns are evaluated and tabulated as the Design Grid, which is a matrix of Principles and Practices of design thinking. Later in this chapter, a generic overview of each principle and practice is provided.

---

13 Martin, R. (2009), *The Design of Business,* Harvard Business Press.

HEURISTICS OF DESIGN THINKING

In the context of Consulting, practitioners can exploit existing knowledge from conventional consulting or explore knowledge for contemporary consulting; while these combinations are at best incremental innovations, the disruptive determinant is in Design Thinking.

- In case of mystery of hypothesis, the exploration required is an early validation from the end customer and extended customer's perspective.

- In case of mystery of stakeholders, the exploration required is interaction with employees, who run the day-to-day operations, those who are best aware of the real causes for current problems and can realistically assess the impact of any proposed solutions.

- In case of mystery of assumptions, the exploration required means to validate at least the critical assumption either by engaging stakeholders across the organization or by testing the assumptions with the extended stakeholders.

- In the case of mystery of interviews, the exploration required is moving away from a rigid question and answer kind of monologue to an open sense and respond kind of dialogue allowing the respondents to freely express their views.

- In case of mystery of the current state, the exploration required is an inclusive evaluation of the context covering the enterprise's ecosystem.

- In case of mystery of target state, the exploration required is an inclusive articulation of the correction considering in-house experiences and internal operations.

- In case of mystery of analysis, the exploration required is a right mix of objective and subjective assessment [i.e.] for every objective finding, the data-point itself needs to be validated first, and then subjectively the impact of the finding to the firm's internal situation.

- In case of mystery of recommendations, the exploration required is the ability to implement balancing business risk and business value, and if need be, by bundling or unbundling recommendations.

'Heuristic' of Design Thinking

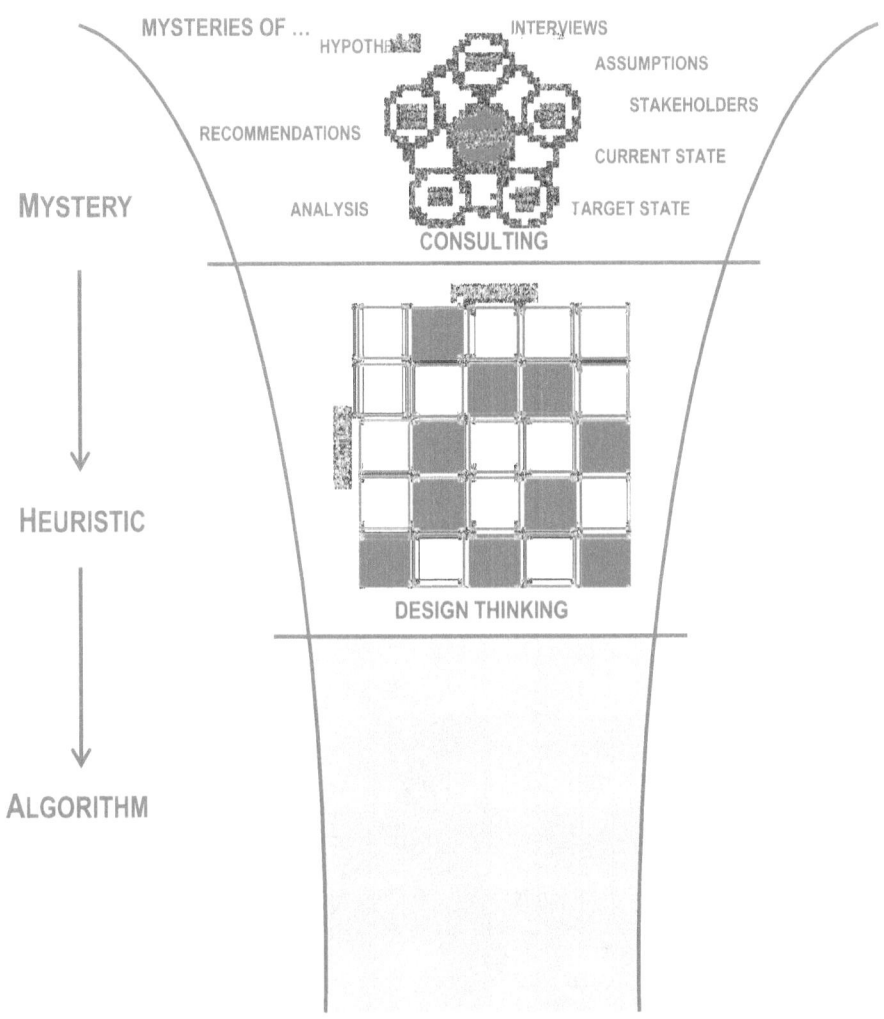

Figure 4-1: Heuristics of Design Thinking

Intertwined in the illustrations above are the 'Principles' and 'Practices' of Design Thinking. Principles are fundamental ideas or general rules that are true regardless of the circumstances, they are the propositions that serve as the foundation for design thinking. Practices on the other hand are the actions, tools, techniques, or processes by which the expected outcomes of the principles are achieved. The matrix of the such principles applicable for consulting in its entirety along with associated practices, is the Design Grid - the heuristic for consulting.

Design Grid

Table 4-1: Design Grid

Practices \ Principles	Human-Centered Design	Embrace Ambiguity & Diversity	Openness to Radical Collaboration	Co-Create Impactful Solutions	Implement & Iteratively Improvise
Empathy Maps	■				
User Personas	■	■			■
How Might We			■		
Storyboarding	■		■		
Interviewing Techniques		■			
Brainstorming		■	■		
Business Model Canvas		■	■		
Journey Maps		■			■
Affinity Diagrams			■	■	
Raskar's Hexagon		■			
Morphological Analysis				■	
Value Proposition Canvas	■				

Design Principles

Principle #1 | Human-Centered Design

Human-centered design, as the name implies is keeping humans/users/customers or simply put people at the core. No matter what we are designing, be a product or a service or a solution or building, we keep our focus intact at the user; empathizing with users, learning more about our users, testing findings with the users, and iterated till the right insights are nailed and ideas made tangible.

The human-centric approach as a design principle can be applied to any field and consulting is no exception. As a consultant interacts with stakeholders, adopting a human-centric approach provides an opportunity to discover not just hard facts, but aspirations, desires, and hidden thoughts and behaviors of our stakeholders, these are insights that conventional information gathering techniques may not yield. Extending beyond information gathering, such insights also help in analyzing and validating findings and iterating early in the consulting cycle to build solutions that resonate with the stakeholders; an opportunity for an early buy-in, and a higher probability of recommendations being accepted.

Principle #2 | Embrace Ambiguity and Diversity

Innovation through iteration is at the core of design thinking, for which there has to be a free flow of ideas, irrespective of whether they are right or wrong. Ambiguity is recognition of this fact, there are multiple variables each with possibly multiple values. Diversity refers to the breadth, of stakeholders, contributors, and critics from varied disciplines. Both ambiguity and diversity are a reality and are essential to design thinking, as they force understanding the problem from multiple perspectives, facilitate an open-minded approach fostering flexibility and thinking from first principles. Implied within, is a need for balance, between not getting lost in the depth of unidirectional solution jumping to conclusions or breadth of omnidirectional outlook getting infinitely stuck in exploring the problem.

In consulting, ambiguity relates to scope and diversity relates to stakeholders. The principle, embracing ambiguity and diversity can be applied to current state assessment or target state definition to understand the diversity of requirements or to Analysis & Findings to acknowledge the ambiguity of findings. Tactfully managing ambiguity and diversity also helps achieve the major objective of alignment and buy-in, the key to the success of the innovation. The involvement of diverse stakeholders thus becomes a pre-requisite to this principle; care should be taken to not allow a multiplicity of ideas to lead to incoherence and create chaos. Practitioners therefore should possess social skills to negotiate and navigate through this dichotomy to overcome such behavioral obstacles and ensure productivity.

PRINCIPLE #3 | OPENNESS TO RADICAL COLLABORATION

Openness to radical collaboration implies learning from diverse perspectives of people from different backgrounds, skills, abilities, and thinking preferences to come together, on contrary traditional collaboration relies on 'so called experts', Radical collaboration embraces multiple perspectives and enables breakthrough insights and solutions to emerge from the diversity, which are the essential ingredients of innovation.

Openness to radical collaboration as a design principle can be applied to consulting as it provides ample opportunities to discover ideas and insights in the context of understanding drivers and incubate innovation in defining the target state. During analysis radical collaboration can come in very handy in identifying unforeseen issues and barriers that may become roadblocks at a later stage, it is a very effective means of identifying potential conflicts and proactively addressing them in the early stages of solutioning.

Radical collaboration is practical in reaching agreements in which all parties feel respected and have their interests met while building long-term relationships, a characteristic that is key to articulating recommendations. Radical collaboration can be practiced with little training and willpower; however, it requires a tremendous amount of openness, curiosity, and perseverance when breaking down barriers between different units. Skills required for radical collaboration are collaborative intent [staying non-defensive and commitment to mutual success], truthfulness, awareness of self and others, and the ability to negotiate through inevitable conflicts, in a way that builds relationships rather than undermining them.

PRINCIPLE #4 | CO-CREATE IMPACTFUL SOLUTIONS

Co-creation stems from active dialogue and well-channeled interaction between stakeholders. Co-creation promotes the emotional engagement of the stakeholders and ensures alignment of diverse perspectives. The participative approach allows stakeholders to free up their inhibitions and freely ideate, because of the trust co-creation fosters. In addition to understanding users' stated needs, co-creation enables the discovery of unmet needs and opportunities to convert them into real opportunities.

In co-creation, the ability to assemble and work with heterogeneous teams is key. Though the diverse profiles, broad expertise, and deep experience of the heterogeneous teams can surely identify innovative ideas, co-creation must still be conducted through a dialog between stakeholders without losing focus on end-users. In addition, co-creation must operate strictly within the boundaries of the strategic priorities, strategic directions and executive decisions must be respected at all times. And for co-creation to be effective stakeholders need to be sorted to identify who amongst them would be contributors, observers, and decision-makers for better engagement. Solutions created with such discipline and collective dedication are bound to be impactful.

Co-create impactful solutions as a design principle can be applied to consulting; the practitioners though rich in external knowledge, often spend a lot of time in getting to understand the internal dynamics of the client environment and are under immense pressure to bring out the right ideas at the right time. In such a context, bringing in diverse stakeholders and ideating through unbiased dialogue, characteristic to co-creation, is a boon to practitioners in defining the target state, analysis, and recommendations. By virtue of being part of the solution, stakeholders turn to become evangelists for implementation.

PRINCIPLE #5 | IMPLEMENT AND ITERATIVELY IMPROVISE

In design thinking, the final stage though commonly referred to as a test, implies both test and implement. The uniqueness of design thinking is that as an approach it allows for improvisations even at this stage as long as they are incremental in nature. Furthermore, if it is beyond incremental and tending to be radical or disruptive, the approach still does not abandon the idea but recommends restart from ideation. What this principle provides for, is to see how the prototype performs and pro-actively workaround the perceived shortcomings iteratively, in order to avoid any last-minute glitches in the product or service.

In consulting, engagements end with a set of recommendations, seldom do they talk of implementation. In some cases, recommendations come with a rationale for implementation expressed in terms of a reward for action and/or the risk of inaction, yet they are not enough to inspire implementation. It is in this context, that a principle like implement and iteratively improvise resonates with practitioners, as it removes inhibitions to implement for fear of failure on the part of clients and provides protection for both in the window of improvisation even post-implementation.

Design Practices

Practice #01 | Empathy Maps

Empathy Maps are a simple yet powerful tool that captures knowledge about a single user or segment of users' behaviors and needs. An empathy map is a 2x2 matrix where each quadrant is labeled with a category that explores the user's external, observable world, and internal mindset; what the user is Saying, Doing, Thinking, and Feeling [includes pains and gains].

In the consulting context, empathy maps can help synthesize observations about client stakeholders and reveal deeper insights about client's needs. When included at the early stages of consulting, empathy maps can help to look at things from the client's point of view before proposing solutions or finalizing recommendations. Empathy maps can also be tactfully used during the consulting cycle, as and when new data and facts become available, empathy maps can be revisited to create new empathy map's, enabling more holistic recommendations that address documented needs as well as needs/traits/demands that are embedded deep inside the client organization but not apparent to leadership.

The first step in an empathy map is to define the person or group of persons to understand and empathize with and identify desired outcomes. Next, capture the outside world, what do they see, what do they hear, what do they do or say. Then, explore the inside mind, what really matters to the users, the positives and negatives of their thoughts, what makes them feel good or bad, explore the specifics of their pains and gains, what is success and failure to the users. Finally, summarize findings, take a moment to reflect, capture ideas and insights generated, take pictures to capture the moment.

Practice #02 | User Personas

A persona in human-centered design is the characterization of a user who represents a segment of the target audience. A user persona is a representation of the goals, desires, limitations, and behavior of a hypothesized group of users. In most cases, personas are synthesized from data collected from interviews with users; details include behavior patterns, goals, skills, attitudes, and the environment, with a few fictional personal details to make the persona a realistic character.

In consulting, especially in understanding context, user personas help to better infer what a real person might need, which can further help in brainstorming, use case specification, and features definition. Once established, proposed solutions can be guided by how well they meet the needs of individual user personas and deliver value. In fact, personas are used as a reference throughout the project lifecycle to ensure that every decision is made in service of the persona's needs that are identified.

Personas can be developed in many ways; common steps are collecting basic demographics, background information of target audience, segmenting the target audience, goals motivations, and pains of the target audience, and additional information like skills, brands, influences, and social networks.

Practice #03 | 'How Might We' Technique

Synthesizing insights from a human-centered approach to problem-solving into actionable statements, by pre-fixing 'How Might We' [[HMV] is the crux of this practice. Meaningful insights generate several HMW statements and each one of them may provide one or more design opportunities, which in turn can lead to a healthy brainstorming session.

In the consulting context, HMW statements can be a powerful means of extracting action items that can address one or more insights. More critical to consulting because every phase throw's up more and more insights that would require logical and sequential evaluation as they shape the next stage. Therefore, techniques such as HMW statements come in handy as they aid in generating a series of options for action and in prioritizing/combining insights into initiatives that help achieve engagement objectives.

In practice, just start by prefixing HMW to an insight, if the insight reads, "users are confused to see many choices", then a good how might we question can be "How might we reduce the number of choices with our users". Having the question reframed, answer by providing ideas, opportunities, or options. Ensure that the number of options is reasonably adequate. Compile all solution options and baseline them for a brainstorming session.

Practice #04 | Storyboarding

Storyboards help to visualize ideas, they capture attention, provide clarity and inspire stakeholders to act. Storyboards communicate a story through images displayed in a sequence of panels that chronologically map the main events of a story. Storyboards are simple and quite basic in nature which makes them easy to understand and very powerful at the same time. Storyboards are of low-fidelity and can be used as an informal means to decision making, they lack details hence must be used in conjunction with other design thinking tools such as user journey maps, empathy maps for optimal results.

Storyboards are a powerful means of ideation. Storyboards sketch out an idea to depict how a user or a team may use a feature or experience an environment or realize a benefit in the future even before starting development work. They bring clarity on the future state and help establish consensus amiong stakeholders at all levels. Storyboards do wonders in choosing the best-suited solution for the organization in the long term, when faced with multiple viable options or directions, filtering out options that do not fit well in the larger solution. All the usages stated are characteristic of any consulting engagement, leverage of the same is almost mandatory for any successful execution.

Storyboards have three broad components, the first component deals with Scenario Planning – The person or user or a team that plays a role in a scenario or a story is clearly specified at the top of the storyboard, with a short text description of the scenario, that is simple enough for a team member or stakeholder to understand what is depicted even before looking at the visual. The second component is the actual Visuals – Each step or phase in the scenario is represented visually in a chronological sequence. The steps can be hand-drawn sketches, or illustrations, or images. Storyboard images are generally quick, low-fidelity drawings to elaborate basic facts, in some cases details relevant to the scenario using speech bubbles. The third component is the Caption – Each visual has a caption, describing the user's actions, environment, experience, feelings, etc. In storyboarding, the image is the primary content, captions, therefore, have to be concise and precise.

PRACTICE #05 | INTERVIEWING TECHNIQUES

In interviewing a set of questions are asked and responses are recorded, a very simplistic definition, but the success of any interview depends on converting this process into a meaningful conversation wherein the stakeholders are comfortable. Making the interviewee at ease helps to have a deeper conversation with the possibility of more meaningful insights as to the outcome. It's a proven practice to ask an open-ended question before asking yes-no type questions. Interviews are categorized into two types – Expert Interviews and Group Interviews. Expert interviews are one-on-one conversations with subject matter experts, to understand the subject, structure, systems, success factors, or show-stoppers and scenarios for the future. In Group interviews, interviewers get a chance to observe the interviewee's behavior, agreements, or disagreements in action, instead of relying only on responses. The flip side is the restriction in a free flow of thoughts.

Interviews are at the heart of consulting and in every phase of the engagement. Talking to stakeholders in understanding context, subject matter experts in assessing the current state, and in defining the target state. Choosing the right technique relevant to the context, customizing the question bank dynamically based on insights captured or because of noticeable discomfort, and maintaining minutes for forward integration or backward traceability becomes key.

In conducting expert interviews, it is critical to choose the right expert, requires research to find the right expert and getting time, asking the right questions to make the best use of the limited time available, and capturing not just the responses, but also the explicit and implicit messages. In conducting group interviews, care should be taken in designing groups, diversity in background and experience to bring out different points of view, having an observer to effectively capture the group's voices and body language. A source for subtle messages that can further add value and lastly ensuring that everyone is engaged by asking direct questions or making more vocal members recede for a moment.

Practice #06 | Brainstorming

Brainstorming is a creative problem-solving technique wherein ideas and solutions are generated through intensive and orchestrated group discussions, a proven method to tap into a broader body of knowledge of multiple individuals. Brainstorms work best when the group is positive, optimistic, and focused on generating as many ideas as possible without any hidden fears or resistance. The key to effective brainstorming is choosing the right group and orchestrating the session. In choosing the group, invite the right people with the right skills for an open discussion, the more diverse the skill set, the more diverse the background of individuals within the group, the better it is to present points/counter-points to make the discussion more productive. In orchestrating the session, there should be ways to control the discussion and steer it in the right direction at all times. Failure to do so can kill the creativity of the group, divert the focus, and consume an awful lot of time. The focus of brainstorming should be to generate as many ideas as possible. The goal isn't a perfect idea, it's lots of ideas, collaboration, and openness to radical thinking.

In consulting, all the above characteristics of brainstorming come into play during the course of any engagement. Stakeholders with diverse backgrounds to interpret the drivers in understanding context, focus groups to accurately baseline the current state, generating of ideas to define the target state, openness in discussion to analyze the findings to determine the feasibility of solution options, and collaboratively converging to shape the recommendations.

In brainstorming, the moderator must ensure an environment of mutual respect and discipline. Tips to set the right tone for a brainstorming session:

1. Do not judge immediately – You never know who can provide the right idea, be open-minded, let everyone contribute freely to what comes to their mind.

2. Encourage radical thinking – Allow the group to think about wild solutions and ideas that can challenge the existing paradigm and give rise to solution leaps.

3. Stay focused – Try not to deviate from the core discussion topic, discuss one topic at a time and move to the next topic only when the previous topic is logically closed.

4. Allow collaboration – Let the group build upon each other's ideas, this is an effective way to select the ideas/solutions that have true potential.

5. Be visual – Allow the group to put forth their ideas in form of images/diagrams or points, enables everyone to comprehend and contribute in real-time.

6. Encourage stepping-up – Invite everyone to go on to the drawing board and freely express themselves to contribute to new ideas or challenge existing ideas.

7. Create lots of ideas – Do not wait for the perfect idea or solution, the aim is to generate as many new ideas as possible, every idea may have the potential to shape the eventual solution.

Practice #07 | Business Model Canvas

The business model describes how an organization generates value for itself and its customers. In practical terms, a business model is a visual articulation of what products and services an organization offers, to whom it offers, how it offers, and how it generates value. In the past, there have been many tools and techniques to articulate a business model from a set of simple statements to high-end visualization of all the steps of the business. One of these tools, which has gained global recognition, is Business Model Canvas, developed by Alexander Osterwalder & Yves Pigneur [14].

The business model canvas is a tool, which helps visualize any business as compactly as possible on a piece of paper. The business model canvas describes any business based on 9 essential building blocks. The 9 essential building blocks are positioned logically in such a way that each interface between the blocks carries a business meaning and taken together describes how an organization generates value. The 9 essential building blocks are – Customer Segments, Value Proposition, Channels, Customer Relationships, Revenue Stream, Key Resources, Key Activities, Key Partnerships, and Cost Structure.

---

14 Osterwalder, A. & Pigneur, Y. (2010), *Business Model Generation*, Wiley India Pvt. Ltd.

In the context of consulting, business model canvas helps to establish a common language among the stakeholders pertaining to the nine building blocks and their relevance across phases. In the current state assessment, it captures customer insights at a high level, shifting the perspective to determine the envisaged business change. In target state definition, the model describes the rationale as to how the organization will create, deliver and measure the value. In analysis and findings, it poses 'what-if' questions to facilitate the creation of better prototypes. In the report and recommendations, the framework assists in envisioning the organization's business model in short, medium, and long-term horizons.

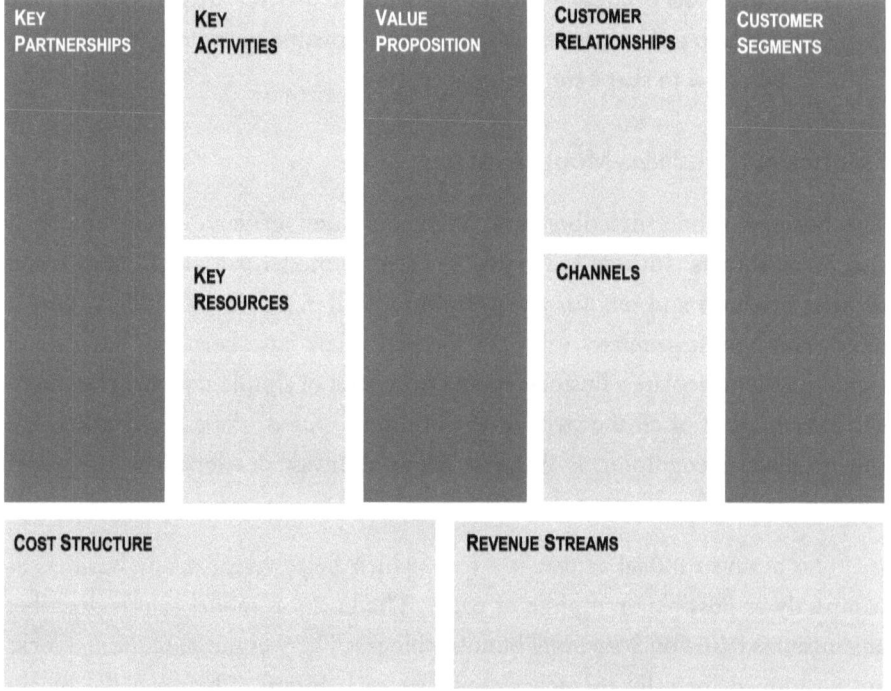

Figure 4-2: Business Model Canvas

BUILDING THE BUSINESS MODEL CANVAS

1. Customer Segments, building block defines the different groups of people or an organization an enterprise aims to reach and serve. Information is captured on parameters like geographic, demographic, social profile, the rationale for the purchase.

2. Value Proposition, building block describes the bundle of products and services that create value for a specific customer segment. Helps define what need is fulfilled or problem the company is going to solve what is the gain that the company is going to create.

3. Channels, building block describes how a company communicates and reaches its customer segments to deliver a value proposition, includes both physical and virtual channels.

4. Customer Relationships, building block describes the types of relationships a company establishes with its specific customer segments. Relationships are driven by the motivation to acquire/retain customers, boost sales, and are surrounded by value, channels, and customers.

5. Revenue Stream, building block represents the cash a company generates from each customer segment [costs must be subtracted from revenues to create earnings]. Avenues to generate revenue streams are asset sales, usage fee, subscription fee, licensing, leasing fee, also include any virtual or indirect value that is created for the company.

6. Key Resources, building block describes the most important assets required to make a business model work, could be financed, physical resources such as manufacturing plant or a store, or intellectual property and patents or even human resources.

7. Key Activities, building block describes the most important things a company must do to make its business model work, includes activities of partners, categorized as production, problem-solving, and platform/network.

8. Key Partnerships, building block describes the network of suppliers and partners that make the business model work, can be a joint venture or a strategic alliance partnership. The motivation for creating partnerships is optimization and economies of scale, reduction of risk, and uncertainty.

9. Cost Structure, building block describes all costs incurred to operate a business model. Structures are drive either by cost or value, characteristics include fixed costs vs variable costs, economies of scale vs economies of scope.

Practice #08 | Journey Maps

Journey maps also referred to as experience maps, are a very powerful tool that provides stakeholders and product teams with a detailed understanding of the user so that they can ideate, prototype, test, and create a meaningful user-centered design. Journey maps systematically go through the steps that customers take both internal and external whilst interacting with a product or service. Given that, it's practically is impossible to map the journey of all users, the creation of a persona helps. A persona is created for one person that best represents the target customer segment. The number of personas required to be created is based on business needs, in most cases, it's one persona per customer segment. Persons that best fit the personas are engaged in fact-finding discussions to understand his/her interactions with the product or service and their motivations.

In the context of consulting, journey maps help empathize with customers or end-users, provide a bigger picture and reveal the right opportunities. Specifically, in the current state assessment journey maps layout touchpoints with the product or service and highlight opportunities for improvement. Journey maps can also be created for the desired target state based on interactions with personas, which can be used to reflect on the current state and identify the gaps to be bridged. Together these journey maps provide an inside-out and outside-in perspective of personas interaction with the product or service, which can indirectly help in analysis and recommendations.

Journey mapping must be conducted with well-defined goals. First, identify the business goal that the journey map will support. Clearly establish who will use the journey maps and for what purpose. Once the goals are defined the journey mapping should be a collaborative process. Many a time, more than the output, the process of journey mapping is more valuable as it provides a real-time view of how customers engage, necessitating the right stakeholders to be invited for data collection. Data thus collected and observations from interactions with personas are key to journey mapping; therefore, they need to be synthesized completely and understood well prior to creating a visual.

Practice #09 | Affinity Diagrams

Affinity diagrams are a great visual tool to help you make sense of mixed data gathered through various sources such as ethnographic research, ideas from

'Heuristic' of Design Thinking

brainstorming, user opinions, user needs, insights, and design issues. Affinity diagrams or clustering exercises are all about organizing data into groups or themes based on their relationships.

Affinity diagrams are one of the most valuable practices of design thinking and can be applied across different phases of consulting. Information gathering is a continuous process in consulting, from understanding context to current state assessment to target state definition to analysis and findings, the information gathered is interpreted and inferences made at every stage resulting in logical groups leading to deeper insights. Affinity diagrams help in the deeper definition of problems and in developing ideas for solutions, steering analysis based on the synthesis of insights.

A simple affinity diagram can be created by the following steps:

1. Note pieces of data, small documented facts, drawings, ideas, and observations onto post-it notes.

2. Take one post-it and make it the first post-it in the first group.

3. Take the next post-it and ask, "Is this similar to the first one or is it different?". Then, you will place it in the first group or into its own group, continue with the rest of the post-its'.

4. You should now have 3-10 groups, name these groups, create information structure, and discover themes.

5. Rank the most important groups over the less important groups. Depending on user priorities, markets, company, and stakeholders.

6. Create connections with other groups using lines or other devices between individual bits of data or groups of data.

7. Summarize what you have synthesized, for example, insights, user needs, pain points, or look for gaps you haven't addressed yet.

Practice #10 | Raskar's Hexagon

Raskar's hexagon or idea hexagon is a framework for arriving at new ideas from a given idea. At the core of using the idea, the hexagon is a need of having a novel and convincing idea or solution, that successfully addresses a genuine problem.

Once the right idea or solution is crystallized, Raskar's hexagon can then help arrive at new ideas stemming out of that particular idea or solution.

In the context of consulting, Raskar's hexagon can help take ideas and solutions to the next level as well as generate new ideas. The solution or an approach or even a concept can be extended using the idea hexagon to benefit the larger enterprise, especially in transformational kind of engagements where the scope extends beyond on consulting segment. The risk, however, is the high degree of emphasis given to the starting idea or solution.

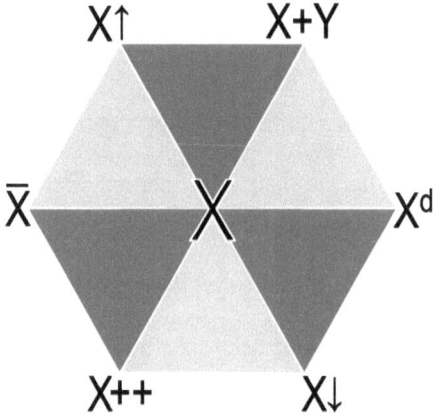

Figure 4-3: Raskar's Hexagon

Raskar's hexagon provides six methods of arriving at a new idea. If the idea is X, what should be the next?

1. X^d Extending the idea to another dimension, raise the complexity of the domain of your idea.

2. X+Y Combining two contrasting ideas and imagining their combination. The more diverse and unrelated the fields are, the more interesting the generated idea will be.

3. X⁻ Doing exactly the opposite of what is currently being thought of right now.

4. X↑ Finding every possible problem that the idea can solve. When an idea solves a problem, it is possible that the same idea can solve many others, too.

5. X↓ Finding every possible solution to the problem. Once a solution to a problem is conceptualized, do not stop but think of more ways to solve it.

6. X++ Adding an adjective to the idea. Making the idea more useful more effective.

PRACTICE #11 | MORPHOLOGICAL ANALYSIS

Morphological Analysis is a creative problem-solving technique for systematically structuring and exploring all possible solutions to a multi-dimensional, complex problem and a powerful tool for generating creative ideas and designing a new product or service. The objective is to break down the system, product, or process problem at hand into its essential parameters or dimensions and to place them in a multi-dimensional matrix. Then find new ideas by searching the matrix for creative and useful combinations. Imagine you have a product that could be made of 3 types of material, in 6 possible shapes, and with 4 kinds of mechanism. Theoretically, there are 72 [3x6x4] potential combinations of material, shape, and mechanism. Some of these combinations may already exist; others may be impossible or impractical. Those leftovers may represent prospective new products. This method can be extended virtually to any problem area that can be structured dimensionally.

In the context of consulting, the practice's ability to evolve at all possible solutions for complex problems is a much-wanted algorithm. Despite the best efforts in understanding context and assessing the current state, when it comes to defining the target state and analysis of findings, there are still a plethora of possibilities. The morphological analysis helps in structuring such possibilities, leading to uncovering innovative solutions.

Illustrative approach to the Morphology Analysis:

1. Define the problem in a short and clear statement.

2. Identify attributes or determine suitable problem characteristics or parameters.

3. Identify alternatives and features for the different parameters, fill a grid with lists of alternatives.

4. Combing items from the lists, identify a new useful, interesting, or potential combination within the grid, and eliminate those combinations that are impossible or undesirable to execute.

5. Evaluate and select ideas to use or develop into practical solutions to the problem.

PRACTICE #12 | VALUE PROPOSITION CANVAS

The value proposition describes how well an organization's products and services fit the market. Value proposition goes hand in hand with the business model, however, the key objective of the value proposition is to deeply assess the fitment between an organization's offerings and customer's needs. There are several ways to define the value proposition for an organization from simple statements to visual techniques. One of the most recognized tools to define value proposition is Value Proposition Canvas, developed by Alexander Osterwalder & Yves Pigneur [15].

The Value Proposition Canvas focuses on two blocks of the business model canvas, which are 'Value Proposition' and 'Customer Segments'. The value proposition canvas maps these two building blocks in order to assess the strength of fitment between the two building blocks. For each customer segment, a 'Customer Profile' is created to better understand the nature of that segment. Based on each customer profile value propositions are mapped to create a 'Value Map'.

Customer Profile is a simple map with three components to better describe and understand, study customers in an actionable way. The three components are as follows:

- Customer Jobs, describe the work or tasks that the customers are trying to be done

- Customer pains, describe anything that annoys customers, creates hurdles that hold them back from getting their job done well.

- Customer gains, describe the outcomes and benefits that get materialized while getting their job done.

---

15 Osterwalder, A. Pigneur, Y. Bernarda, G. & Smith, A. (2014), *Value Proposition Design*, Wiley India Pvt. Ltd.

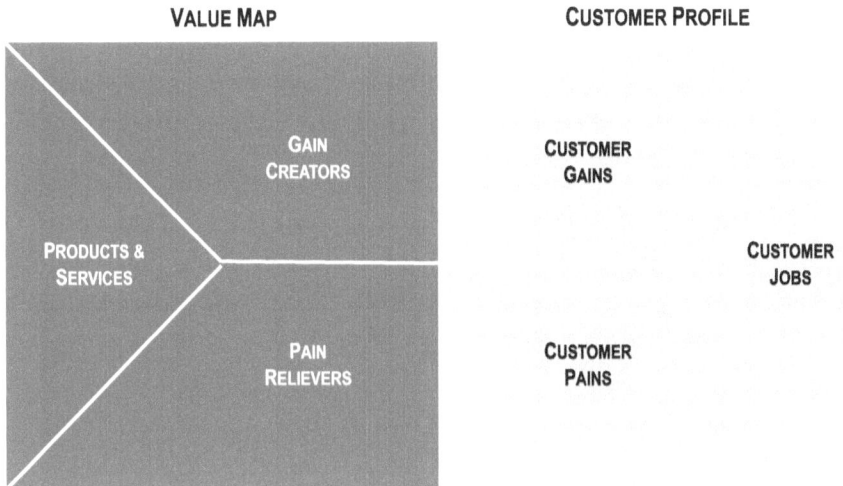

Figure 4-4: Value Proposition Canvas

Value Map, describes the features of a specific value proposition in your business model in a more structured and detailed way, it breaks the value map into:

- Products & Services, are the offerings that help customers complete their job. Products could be physical and tangible, or intangible. It is important to understand the relevance of each product or service to your customers.

- Pain Relievers, describe how exactly the products and services relieve customer pains while helping customers get their job done. Pain relievers can be unique features of Products & Services that simplify customer's jobs.

- Gain Creators, describe how exactly the products and services create gains that really matter to customers. Like pain relievers, gain creators are unique features of products & services that help achieve customers the right benefits.

The final step in Value Proposition Canvas is the fitment between Customer Profile and Value Map. The most effective products and services are when they get the customer's job done, alleviate maximum possible pains, and create gains that really matter to the customers. It may not be practically possible to relieve all pains and ensure all gains. However, the value proposition canvas helps achieve an optimal fitment, which can make customers happy and business sustainable.

Key Learnings

Heuristics guide us toward a solution by way of organized exploration of the possibilities, they represent an incomplete yet distinctly advanced understanding of what was previously a mystery.

In the Design Grid, the mysteries of consulting are evaluated and tabulated as a matrix of Principles and Practices. Principles are fundamental ideas or general rules that are true regardless of the circumstances. Practices are the actions, tools, techniques, or processes by which the expected outcomes of the principles are achieved.

Principles in the context of the heuristic of consulting are – Human-centered design, embracing ambiguity and diversity, openness to radical collaboration, co-creating impactful solutions, and implementing and iteratively improvising. The associated practices are – Empathy Maps, User Personas, How Might We, Storyboarding, Interviewing Techniques, Brainstorming, Business Model Canvas, Journey Maps, Affinity Diagrams, Raskar's Hexagon, Morphological Analysis, and Value Proposition Canvas.

Intersections of the above principles and practices become the heuristic of consulting. the pattern to explore algorithms for design thinking in consulting.

. Ω .

Part Three

Design Thinking in Consulting

Chapter 5

'Algorithm' for Design Thinking in Consulting

Algorithms are a general way of getting toward the desired solution – into a formula or a set of rules. Algorithms differ from heuristics in that they are certified production processes, that in the absence of intervention or complete anomaly, following the sequence of steps they embody will produce a particular result. Algorithms are more efficient than heuristics, can be run by less experienced and less expensive personal.[16]

Challenging the heuristic patterns of thought, behavior, and feeling, design thinking paves the way to develop algorithms that produce solutions that generate new meanings and activate diverse elements like cognitive, emotional, and sensory, that are involved in the human experience, by understanding cultures, experiences, emotions, thoughts and behavior to provide inspiration to the initiative to succeed and sustain.

In this chapter, the 'Algorithm' for Design Thinking in Consulting is explained, primarily to get a better understanding of the meta-formulae, prior to applying the same for each of the consulting phases and annotating for the consulting segments as applicable.

---

16 Martin, R. (2009), *The Design of Business,* Harvard Business Press.

The Re-imagined Knowledge Funnel

The re-imagined Knowledge Funnel depicts how the algorithm for design thinking in consulting is arrived at, starting the consulting as the mystery followed by design thinking as the heuristic.

Consulting – The Mystery

The route out of a mystery begins with a hunch. Hunches are prelinguistic intuitions.

Intuitions in the context of consulting are; the way the hypothesis is articulated to define the problem statement, the emphasis placed on executive leadership to provide strategic and operational directions, the assumptions made in order to deliver within the short duration of consulting engagements, the completeness of pre-formatted questionnaires used for information gathering, the presumptive notion that something is broken internally and therefore external help is being sought, the inherent tendency that a solution that worked elsewhere will work here also, the reliance on benchmarks to highlight the deviation, the expectation on recommendations to succeed in implementation.

Intuitions expressed above are spread across the consulting phases and may vary depending upon the nature of the consulting segment, hence, they are taken together to be the mystery to be addressed.

Design Thinking – The Heuristic

Heuristics are open-ended prompts to think in a particular way, heuristics offer no guarantee that using them produces a certain result. Heuristics are different from hunches in that they bring intuitions to language.

The heuristic that can best solve the mysteries of consulting as summarized above is design thinking by exploring; requirements from end customers and extended customers point of view, interactions with associates who are close to the problem at hand, early validation of assumptions, inclusive evaluation of enterprise's ecosystem, in-house experiences in articulating corrections, business risk and business value balancing and by bundling or un-bundling recommendations.

'Algorithm' for Design Thinking in Consulting

Heuristics expressed above are exploited in the Design Grid, an innovative technique, based on careful evaluation of principles of design thinking and associated practices that can potentially enhance and extend the consulting solution.

DESIGN THINKING IN CONSULTING – THE ALGORITHM

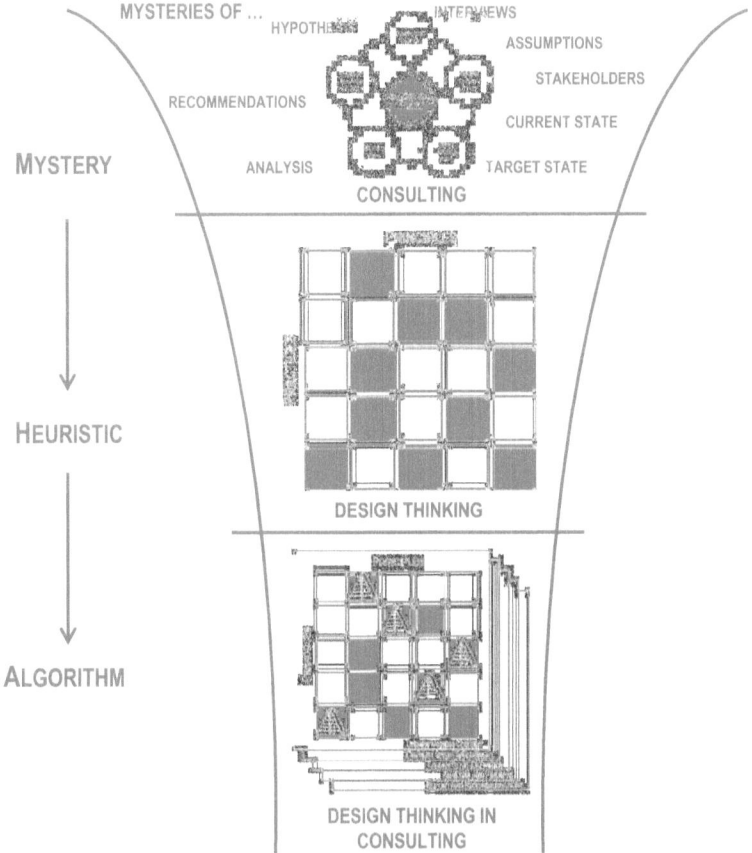

Figure 5-1: Algorithm for Design Thinking in Consulting

The design grid is the starting point for the algorithm. Each principle in the design grid defines 'the what', a characteristic or a contemporary thought of design thinking, that can be applied to consulting and can potentially enhance or enrich the execution of the consulting engagement. And for each principle, there are a set of practices describing 'the how', a tool or technique of design thinking, that helps in achieving the objective of the corresponding principle.

Given that each of the consulting phases is unique, the generic design grid [i.e.] the pattern from the heuristic needs to be evaluated further to derive the phase-specific design grid. This involves the identification of principles applicable to the consulting phase and evaluation of practices associated with the identified principles to short-list practices relevant to the particular consulting phase. The phase-specific design grid is further studied to understand the nuances for each of the consulting segments as applicable, collectively this becomes the formulae or Algorithm for Design Thinking in Consulting.

In the following chapters, the conventional approach for each of the consulting phases is revisited with illustrations for select consulting segments. Opportunities for design thinking are first identified and then the design grid is leveraged, to highlight select principles for that particular phase along with related practices and to explain how a contemporary thought like design thinking is applied. Following which, instantiations that articulate the nuances of application for select consulting segments to fully appreciate the value and impact of design thinking in consulting are provided.

Key Learnings

Algorithms are a general way of getting toward the desired solution – into a formula or a set of rules. Algorithms differ from heuristics in that they are certified production processes. Challenging the heuristic patterns of thought, behavior, and feeling, design thinking paves the way to develop algorithms that produce solutions.

The Algorithm for Design Thinking in Consulting is built by re-imagining the knowledge funnel, wherein the mystery is taken to be the consulting segments across the consulting phases, the heuristic is the pattern for consulting, the design grid, a matrix of principles and practices of design thinking.

The Algorithm is then formulated by evaluating the Design Grid to make it phase-specific and extrapolating further to highlight the nuances of consulting segments.

. Ω .

Chapter 6

Design Thinking in Understanding Context

In Understanding Context, the goal is to get a good grasp of the real problem that is to be solved. In many cases, it may not be apparent and would require intelligent probing to go beyond the hypothesis in order to define the problem statement. Another unique characteristic is that it involves extensive interviewing, therefore identifying the real stakeholders is key, insights from these interviews not only help in firming up the problem statement but also in getting early clues to cause for the current context.

Design Thinking is the perfect antidote, the common trait of design thinking culture is to identify and solve the root causes of the real problem, coupled with a deep understanding of the real stakeholders. Design thinking emphasizes on an empathetic approach to discovering stated plus unarticulated user needs, be it interviews with individuals or brainstorming in groups. The mission of design thinking is to translate these observations into insights and insights into developing real solutions.

In this chapter, Design Thinking as applied to the Understanding Context phase of consulting is explained, starting with an overview of the consulting phase with illustrations for activities across consulting segments, leading to the customization of the Design Grid by selecting relevant Principles and related Practices. These intersections are further detailed as to how they can enrich understanding of the context, including instantiations for select segments of the consulting spectrum.

Understanding Context

Objectives

The objective of the Understanding Context[17] phase is, to understand the client context in terms of the drivers, business, technology, stakeholders, scope, and outcomes.

Key Activities

Understanding Drivers

A genuine understanding of the real drivers is a pre-requisite for developing or designing an effective solution. Helps in gaining insights on the importance of the initiative and the real motive. Need to go beyond the symptoms to unearth the cause, requires trust, diplomacy, probing, and experience sharing.

Illustrations for Understanding Drivers

- In IT Strategy Consulting the drivers are the need to translate corporate strategy or business strategy into IT strategy or develop an IT strategy leveraging innovations in technology for competitive advantage.

- In IT Architecture Consulting the drivers are increasing enterprise system reliability, availability, scalability, or establishing easier communications with external partners, enabling better integration across applications, better management of data, reduction in the redundancy of infrastructure services, heterogeneity of infrastructure components across lines of business.

- In Transformation Consulting the drivers are a change to the business model triggered by external impetus like a merger or acquisition or divestiture, changes in the customer buying behavior or enhancing product mix or advent of new technologies, or because of internal motivations like simplifying the business and operations, improving stakeholder experience or improving operational efficiency.

---

17 Kancharla, M. (2016), *Consulting – A Practitioner's Perspective*, Notion Press.

Understanding Business

A deep understanding of the company's past is essential to assess the present and shape the future. Study the journey right from its inception, taking notes of organizational dynamics like shareholder management, executive accountability, financial performance, mergers and/or acquisitions, products & services, customer satisfaction, growth in terms of size & geographical spread, and work culture. A good source of information is the company's annual reports and website. Additionally, review industry reports to get a sense of industry trends, the client's relative position/standing in the industry, and insights into the competitor world.

Illustrations for Understanding Business

- In IT Architecture Consulting business architecture is the starting point for enterprise architecture, thinking on the above parameters will help get clarity on the expectations of business from IT and implications of the business architecture on application portfolio, technology platform, and infrastructure configuration.

- In IT Portfolio Management studying the business to understand the existing business capability and associated business components, functional coverage of applications, and investment distribution between run the business and change the business. It is equally important to capture non-functional requirements like the availability of mission critical applications.

- In IT Governance Consulting, understand the strategic directions of the enterprise. Is the goal of the enterprise to be profit-oriented, growth-oriented, or a combination of both profit and growth? In the former the focus is on profitability via enterprise wide coordination and core competencies, in the latter, the focus is business unit innovation with only a few mandated processes and for the in-between combination, the focus is on asset utilization [i.e.] efficient operation by maximizing IT sharing and reuse.

Understanding Technology

Understanding technology in terms of how it can best enable a business to transform; would it be through reducing the complexity of the technology stack, rationalization of applications, streamlining of current operations, simplification of governance processes, standardization of processes, or virtualization of infrastructure is critical. Evaluate business needs to determine the guiding principles for IT. Ability to scale will mandate emphasis on transaction processing, information storage, and connectivity, applications not being dependent on the underlying platform, and scalability of infrastructure.

Illustrations for Understanding Technology

- In IT Portfolio Management understand the technology stack in terms of platforms and products, database structures and dependencies, network and communication protocols. Pay special attention to the age of applications, availability of support, and it's potential to sustain.

- In IT Process Consulting understand processes related to the application development process, release management, configuration management, and service management. Group processes into work streams to enable both atomic and aggregate analysis. Analyze the current practices in the prioritized process areas, the opportunity for improvement, and the potential for optimization.

- In IT Infrastructure Consulting understand technology to assess the impact of aging/obsolete technology, out-of-support technology, skillset shortage, regulatory compliance, standardization, and vendor stability.

Understanding Stakeholders

Understanding people is the next logical step following understanding of business and technology. At this stage, the people's study is restricted to the key stakeholders in order to get their collective buy-in. Knowing who your adversaries

Design Thinking in Understanding Context   107

are is as important as who your evangelists are. Both are bound to exist in any context. In all conversations, care should be taken to present one's position and be flexible enough to respect the other's position; the key is to arrive at a common understanding for collective benefit.

ILLUSTRATIONS FOR UNDERSTANDING STAKEHOLDERS

- In IT Governance Consulting the stakeholder set is very varied, extends beyond IT to business, to executive leadership, and occasionally to the board level. Stakeholder management in the context of governance consulting is extremely sensitive, needs to be handled delicately with diplomacy, not being influenced nor being judgmental. The idea is to hear the individual's role, responsibilities in the first person and his/her insights on all other interactions as a third person.

- In IT Process Consulting understanding stakeholders means support from senior stakeholders, an input that is critical to generating momentum and delivering high impact change. The need of the hour is to designate a senior executive as the process sponsor and empower him or her with a pool of process champions. The people who do the work know how to make it work better.

- In IT Outsourcing Consulting the stakeholder set spans across the organization, beyond the conventional IT leaders and associated business owners to the functional heads of human resources, finance, facilities, and even legal. The diversity of this stakeholder set mandates mobilization of subject matter experts in every area, to meaningfully dialog and negotiate, to appreciate each stakeholder's challenges, apprehensions, and expectations, to collaborate and conclude with a convincing business case.

UNDERSTANDING SCOPE & OUTCOMES

Understanding the scope that was stated in the proposal and the statement of work with the engagement sponsor. Seldom are they exact, there will always be variations because of a difference in understanding or interpretation. Be prepared to accommodate for some modifications as they are likely to be revisited and reprioritized. Equally important is to have a common understanding of the outcomes/end deliverables in terms of coverage and depth.

ILLUSTRATIONS FOR UNDERSTANDING SCOPE & OUTCOMES

- In IT Governance Consulting scope of the engagement is a function of the focus areas to be addressed. It could be structure or processes in a stand-alone mode or structure and mechanisms or processes and measurements in combination or collectively all the four focus areas. The expected outcome is ensuring the right structure with corresponding roles and responsibilities, defining authority direction and support for key governance activities, linkage of business and IT plans, right processes along with the key controls, understanding of the enterprise's appetite for risk and compliance requirements and effective change management practices.

- In IT Infrastructure Consulting the scope of an operational infrastructure consulting engagement typically is an assessment of the current state IT infrastructure landscape from a server, storage, network, and security perspective in order to determine and document the future state infrastructure architecture, infrastructure roadmap, cost/benefit analysis and strategies to co-exist while transitioning from the current state to target state.

- In IT Transformation Consulting the scope is a function of the defined transformation imperatives, the selection of the spectrum segment that would be the core and the supporting spectrum segments that would support the core as corollaries, while the outcome of the transformation would be the changed business model.

OUTCOMES

The outcome of this phase is a jointly developed and agreed upon engagement scope, plan, deliverables, detailing out the schedule, intermediate milestones, depth of coverage, dimensions to focus on, frameworks to use, review and approval cycle, final presentation format & target audience, report structure & submission, and governance model for the course of the engagement.

Opportunity for Design Thinking

In general, most of the activities in understanding context are accomplished through review of annual reports, corporate strategy, business strategy, analyst briefings, interviews of key stakeholders, or brainstorming in focus groups. And in all the illustrations, it is the consultants that drive the information gathering process based on their experiences, leveraging their pre-configured questionnaires or pre-tested workshop agendas. In a sense, herein lies the limiting factor of a conventional approach and an opportunity for contemporary thought like design thinking.

Design Thinking in Understanding Context

The Algorithm for Understanding Context is built on the Design Thinking Principles of Human-centered Design and Radical Collaboration.

Human-centered Design

Human-centered design helps in identifying the real problem through interacting with real users and thereby aiding in articulating the right solution. In relation to the key activities of understanding context, this principle is applied primarily to understanding end users of the enterprise and its ecosystem rather than restricting to the echelon of executives. Secondarily, these insights from end users can be leveraged to further understand drivers, business, and technology. Notice the change in order, conventionally it would have been starting with drivers to business to technology, it now starts with end users who are facing the problem and who need the solution.

Design thinking practices that are related to Human-centered design and required for understanding context are Empathy Maps and User Personas.

Empathy Maps

Empathy maps, provide a simple 2x2 visual of what the stakeholders are saying, doing, thinking, and what are their feelings, pains, and gains. Representation of such behaviors based on a human centric approach on an empathy map also helps to get a different perspective of other contextual elements like the drivers, business, and technology.

Table 6-1: Design Grid for Understanding Context

Practices \ Principles	Human-centered Design	Embrace Ambiguity & Diversity	Openness to Radical Collaboration	Co-Create Impactful Solutions	Implement & Iteratively Improvise
Empathy Maps	▲				
User Personas	▲				■
How Might We			▲		
Storyboarding	■		▲		
Interviewing Techniques		■			
Brainstorming		■	■		
Business Model Canvas		■	■		
Journey Maps			■		■
Affinity Diagrams			■	■	
Raskar's Hexagon		■	■		
Morphological Analysis				■	
Value Proposition Canvas	■				

1. INSTANTIATION OF EMPATHY MAP FOR IT GOVERNANCE CONSULTING

   In IT Governance Consulting, stakeholders span across the enterprise. The group that is selected can be a representative sample across the departments with varying levels of seniority.

   The way each of them sees the outer world would vary distinctly, executives might see governance from a regulation perspective; operational heads might see it from a compliance perspective, human resources personnel might see it from a span of control perspective.

   Exploring the inside mind might reveal that executives are adhering to the rule rather than the spirit of the regulation, operational heads are focusing on compliance to the extent required for reporting and not as a way for working, human resources personnel are evaluating span for control to identify potential for greater responsibility.

   Summarizing on the empathy map may provide insights to the real challenge; is it the governance mechanism or governance measure that needs to be addressed, how critical is adherence to regulation for their industry, how to communicate the risk of non-compliance, etc.

2. INSTANTIATION OF EMPATHY MAP FOR IT PROCESS CONSULTING

   In IT Process Consulting, stakeholders should not be restricted to just the operations staff, the selected group should comprise of process champions from across the enterprise led by an empowered process sponsor.

   In this case, the way each member sees the outer world should be the same, the operational efficiency or the improvement on industry benchmark goal set by the organization should be respected and registered by every member.

   Internally, the process sponsor must be willing to appreciate the ground realities, and the process champions in-turn must be willing to understand the real purpose behind the corporate initiative. Only then can the outcome sustain and not fizzle out post being a one-time accomplishment.

   Summarized on the empathy map, it depicts process sponsors saying of the goal and thinking of the rationale for process champions to reflect and act upon, this becomes the doing part and when documented with feelings, it completes the circle of collaboration.

3. INSTANTIATION OF EMPATHY MAP FOR IT OUTSOURCING CONSULTING

In IT Outsourcing Consulting, stakeholders span not just across the enterprise but beyond to system integrators and service providers. The selected group, therefore, should have representatives of business, technology, and operations from each of these entities and more importantly people who perform the liaison roles between the entities.

The outer world, in this case, is nothing but the inner world of each of the entities. While it is acceptable for the stakeholders to be focused on their individual goals, it is equally important to collectively collaborate to achieve the outsourcing outcome.

Internally speaking, the role of liaising stakeholders becomes critical, to extract meaningful contributions from each of the external stakeholders per their subject matter expertise and converge towards the common objective for outsourcing through skillful negotiation.

Summary plotted on an empathy map would depict the diversity of saying, doing, and thinking aspects of each stakeholder for the liaising stakeholder to absorb and act upon, and in doing so, the empathy map also helps in capturing the feelings of this central entity who would be most impacted post outsourcing.

The value of empathy maps is quite evident in the instantiations illustrated above; conventional information gathering techniques like interviewing or questionnaires may provide answers to what stakeholders say or do, but empathy maps help in capturing the additional critical insight of real feelings of real stakeholders and provide a different perspective to revisit and re-understand rest of the information.

USER PERSONAS

User personas help in building up the right profile to understand the context. The profile here can be an individual whose needs are being identified to achieve the organization's business goal or an infrastructure whose specifications are being determined to create the right technology platform or an institution whose capabilities are being evaluated to ensure that they can be trusted service providers.

1. INSTANTIATION OF USER PERSONAS FOR IT STRATEGY CONSULTING

    In IT Strategy Consulting, user personas can play a critical role in better addressing business drivers. Consider a task like strategizing a business goal – how to capture new customer segments, for which the bank would like to understand and attract millennials.

    In order to accomplish the above goal, the conventional approach would mandate the study of existing customer segments, evaluating current products, and extrapolating characteristics of the segments/products to determine the customized product for the new segment.

    On the other hand, developing a user persona would mean developing the characteristics of a typical millennial and what his/her banking needs would be, not in isolation but by interacting with millennials directly in their environment. The developed user persona thus will provide insights like millennials' preference to the internet or mobile banking as opposed to on premise banking, preference for products that make e-Commerce purchasing easier, etc.

2. INSTANTIATION OF USER PERSONAS FOR IT INFRASTRUCTURE CONSULTING

    In IT Infrastructure Consulting, user personas can help in understanding technical specifications to define the infrastructure platform. Consider the task of defining end user communication setup, say for a D2H content provider.

    In a conventional approach, the specifications are defined based on the kind of content that gets transmitted, the speed for the same, and therefore the bandwidth required for uninterrupted streaming.

    On the other hand, user personas focus on the characteristics of the end user environment, the physical characteristic of the premise, and demographic details of the people in the premise like whether the premise is an independent dwelling or condominium or apartment complex or a gated community, and whether the denizens are students or a small family or a large joint-family.

3. INSTANTIATION OF USER PERSONAS FOR IT OUTSOURCING CONSULTING

In IT Outsourcing Consulting, user personas can help in better understanding stakeholders, who could also be institutions like third party service providers. Consider the task of evaluating the cultural fit of an outsourcing service provider.

Conventionally, outsourcing analysis focuses on technical capabilities, cost arbitrage, time-zone advantages, timelines to reach a steady state, operational efficiencies, and adherence to service level agreements.

On the other hand, user personas lay additional focus on cultural aspects, value systems of the service provider that would help in extending the relationship from a simple short-term business relationship to a long-term mutually beneficial relationship; a relationship based on trust.

The value of user personas as evident from the above instantiations is that they facilitate dynamic insights way beyond static information, by creating a profile or a persona. Instantiations reinforced its application to individuals where the insights led to right segmentation and right product design, to the infrastructure where the insights led to additional demographic details and physical characteristics of the premise both which can help in better servicing end-user communication needs and to institutions where the insights led to the importance of cultural characteristics of the service provider and therefore their ability to become a trusted partner.

OPENNESS TO RADICAL COLLABORATION

Openness to radical collaboration mandates reaching out to as diverse a stakeholder set as possible to gain insights that are far reaching in understanding the true context of the engagement. Radical collaboration is very much relevant to understanding context. In fact, radical collaboration is necessary to truly understand business context from business drivers, technology and stakeholders to scope of consulting engagement. The relationships built here can be leveraged further into the subsequent phases of consulting.

Design thinking practices that are related to radical collaboration and required for understanding context are, 'How Might We' Technique, and Storyboarding.

'How Might We' Technique

The crux of this practice is to pre-fix 'How Might We' [HMW] in every collaboration to every discussion, the idea is to draw diverse insights from the diverse stakeholders and debate further on their implications and impact. The practice can support all the activities of Understanding Context and therefore is in total alignment with the principle of radical collaboration.

1. Instantiation of 'How Might We' Technique for IT Strategy Consulting

    In IT Strategy Consulting, the HMW technique can be quite handy in understanding drivers. Consider the task of translating the organization's business strategy to IT strategy.

    In order to address a business goal like, 'Reduction in operational expenses by a certain percentage, year on year', a conventional approach would be to evaluate transactional and operational costs and explore ways to reduce operational expenses, say by downsizing infrastructure and/or workforce.

    Prefixing HMW to the above reasoning will allow for diverse insights that can be further debated. The goal of reduction in operational expenses by a certain percentage can be paraphrased as 'How might we reduce the cost to income ratio'. The resulting responses might give additional insights into revisiting cost structures – be it through an increase in productivity, efficiency in operations, rationalization of applications, or virtualization of infrastructure.

2. Instantiation of 'How Might We' Technique for IT Architecture Consulting

   In IT Architecture Consulting, the HMW technique can be leveraged to understanding business. Consider the task of deriving the application architecture from the business architecture.

   The conventional approach to build application architecture based on the business architecture would be to evaluate the existing business functions of the enterprise and cross-verify for supporting systems or applications to support the same. This approach follows a one-to-one mapping path for a given business function what are the required IT applications.

   Prefixing HMW to the exploration of business architecture will facilitate additional insights. A simplistic statement such as 'How might we enhance IT capability to address the business drivers', will yield additional capabilities required from IT which could span across multiple functions, this ensures completeness of the application architecture and better co-relation to the business architecture.

3. Instantiation of 'How Might We' Technique for IT Portfolio Management

   In IT Portfolio Management, the HMW technique can be applied to better understand the IT portfolio. Consider the task of deciding on improving the health of the application portfolio.

   In such analysis, typically only the existing parameters like age of application, the stability of the application, availability of support are considered [i.e.] future decisions being articulated based on present conditions.

   Prefixing HMW to assessing the health of the application portfolio can be paraphrased as 'How might we improve the efficiency of business intelligence applications of the portfolio' or 'How might we increase the budgets for growing the business applications and reduce budgets for run the business applications'. Though these statements are at a macro level, they can trigger ideas and insights at a micro level, when combined can deliver viable solution options that can alter the health of the application portfolio.

4. INSTANTIATION OF 'HOW MIGHT WE' TECHNIQUE FOR IT GOVERNANCE CONSULTING

   In IT Governance Consulting, the HMW technique can be of major help in understanding stakeholders. Consider the task of synthesizing stakeholders' sense of the problem and suggestions for the solution.

   Conventionally, stakeholders are interviewed in separate sessions as per their rank or as per their responsibility, Therefore, the questions from the consultant are targeted at one particular stakeholder set and the response would obviously mean an individual opinion.

   Prefixing HMV to the above information gathering would make the questions read as 'How might we seek the collective insights of all stakeholders' or 'How might we get to know the customer's perspective of the real problem and or required solutions.

5. INSTANTIATION OF 'HOW MIGHT WE' TECHNIQUE FOR IT TRANSFORMATION CONSULTING

   In the context of IT Transformation Consulting, the HMW technique is best suited to understand the scope of the engagement. Consider the task of determining what consulting segment should be at the core and what should be the corollary segments to be considered.

   Ironically in many a case, this gets pre-determined by the buying group of the consulting services and the practice that prospected the opportunity in the first place, resulting in an inherent bias from both sides.

   Prefixing HMW would mean transforming the probe to read as 'How might we identify the real cause for the current transformation need' or 'How might we identify the impacted areas to investigate and their inter-dependencies'.

The benefit of the HMW technique lies in the fact that it expands the scope of solution search and span of the stakeholder set, just by prefixing HMW to the original ask. HMW statements increase the breadth of the question, seek diversity of audience including end customers in a collective and collaborative way, and enable reframing the problem statement to achieve a larger goal to realize a sustainable solution.

STORYBOARDING

Understanding Context being the starting point, almost everything other than the drivers for the engagement is unknown. Rightful understanding of the drivers is key to accurate interpretation of the business need, technology implications, onboarding the competent consultants, and identifying stakeholders that matter and can contribute material. Strange as it may sound, simple techniques can actually best solve complex problems and storyboarding is one such practice. Storyboarding is simple visual, articulated through radical collaboration covering a cross-section of the business drivers.

1. INSTANTIATION OF STORYBOARDING FOR IT TRANSFORMATION CONSULTING

   In IT Transformation Consulting, the drivers are complex and interwoven, the impact is one to many. Consider the task of understanding drivers in a transformational program like a merger of two auto manufacturers.

   In the conventional approach, the emphasis shifts quickly to the integration plan, focusing only on the listed work items and getting things done for the go-live date. Therefore, the priority becomes ensuring system availability and business continuity without clearly understanding the purpose of the combined entity.

   Storyboarding is a simple technique that starts from first principles and enables the big picture to evolve through simple images along with captions for the different scenarios that collectively portray the true purpose of the combined entity.

The advantage of the storyboard is that in small bites through simple images the story evolves, starting with the ask to expectation from business, technology, and stakeholders. Though this is enormous in literal terms, the visual nature of representation and that too in one frame makes it valuable for every stakeholder to absorb the big picture and also to get a sense of every cause and effect.

Design Thinking in Understanding Context

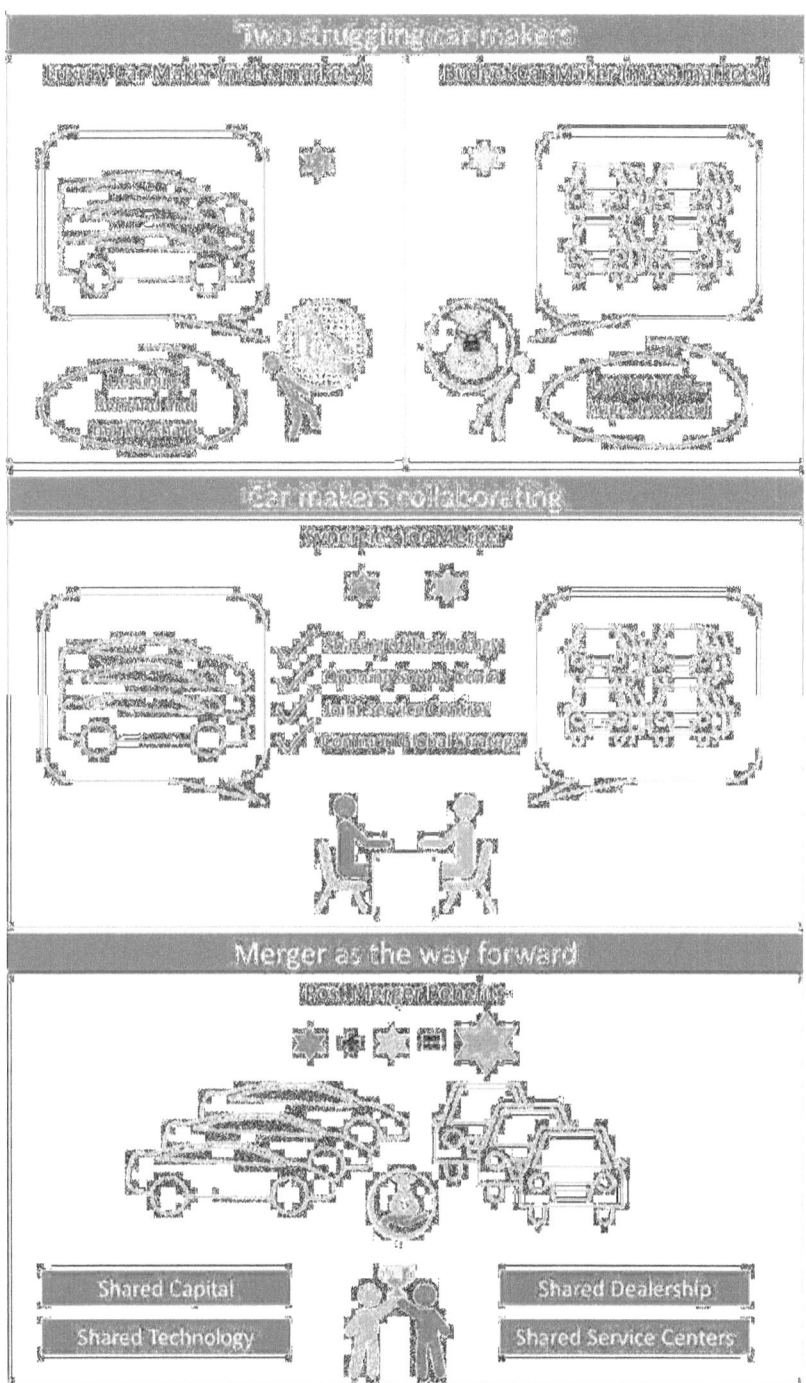

Figure 6-1: Storyboarding

Outcomes of Design Thinking

As evident from the instantiations across the consulting spectrum for the same set of activities of understanding context, design thinking principles direct the understanding to be more human-centered and enable broadening of insights through radical collaboration. Furthermore, the underlying practices help in capturing the additional critical insights, be it the real feelings of real stakeholders through empathy maps or the additional demographic and dynamic data gathered through user personas or the expansion of solution search by prefixing HMW or the simple summary that the storyboard offers to absorb the big picture. The real value, however, comes from how this alternative and/or augmented insights become a force-multiplier in the remaining phases of the consulting engagement.

Key Learnings

Key activities of understanding context are understanding the drivers for change, business environment, technology ecosystem, stakeholders, scope, and outcomes. Understanding context is the first phase of the consulting cycle and because of which the context is bound to be blurred. Yet the expectation is to arrive at an accurate understanding as the information and insights gained at this stage are critical for all the subsequent phases.

In the conventional approach information gathering is driven, primarily by the consultant's expertise and the assets/accelerators of the advisory firm. This approach runs the risk of being unable to reach out to the real stakeholder, being unable to articulate the real problem.

The mitigation lies in design thinking, a contemporary thought that emphasizes an empathetic approach to discovering stated plus unarticulated user needs, be it interviews with individuals or brainstorming in groups. The mission of design thinking is to translate these observations into insights and insights into developing real solutions.

Principles relevant to understanding context are Human-centered design and Radical collaboration. Human-centered design helps in identifying the real problem through interacting with real users and then leveraging these insights to understand drivers, business, and technology. Radical collaboration mandates reaching out to as diverse a stakeholder set as possible to gain insights that are far reaching in understanding the true context of the engagement.

Practices related to human-centered design and required to understand context are Empathy maps and User personas. Empathy maps provide a simple 2x2 visual of what the stakeholders are saying, doing, thinking, and what are their feelings, pains, and gains. User personas help in building up the right profile to understand the context, the profile here can be an individual, infrastructure, or institution.

Practices related to radical collaboration and required to understand context are How Might We Techniques and Storyboarding. In the HMW technique, the idea is to draw diverse insights from diverse stakeholders and debate further on their implications and impact. Storyboarding is a simple technique that starts from first principles and enables the big picture to evolve through simple images along with captions for the different scenarios that collectively portray the real requirement.

The above four practices have been applied to illustrative activities across the consulting spectrum; the instantiations demonstrated the relevance of the practices and principles of design thinking and the value that practitioners can derive through design thinking in understanding context.

. Ω .

Chapter 7

Design Thinking in Current State Assessment

In the Current State Assessment, the goal is to assess the as-is elements across the enterprise as per the agreed upon scope of the engagement. The assessment could potentially include some or all of the following; the organization context in light of the concern being addressed, its position vis-à-vis the market/competition, the business in terms of the products and/or services the organization offers, the technology and infrastructure that supports the business, the processes that the organization operates with, the structures and mechanisms that the organization is governed by, and last but not the least the people and cultural aspects of the organization. While all these elements are internal to the enterprise, equally important is the assessment of the external elements like industry regulations and market dynamics as they could have been the cause of the problem or can influence the solution to the problem.

Design Thinking is the perfect approach as the coverage required for the assessment is both broad and deep, requiring a clear focus on when to pause, respecting the views of diverse stakeholders. Characteristics of design thinking that can complement current state assessment are; information gathering that is divergent, ideation that is cumulative, incrementally building on each idea without rejecting any, inclusivity in reach out to end customers, and extraction of the unmet needs even from the extreme users.

In this chapter, Design Thinking as applied to the Current State Assessment phase of consulting is explained, starting with an overview of the consulting phase with illustrations for activities across consulting segments, leading to the customization of the Design Grid by selecting relevant Principles and related Practices. These intersections are further detailed as to how they can enhance current state assessment, including instantiations for select segments of the consulting spectrum.

Current State Assessment

Objectives

The objective of the Current State Assessment[18] phase is to baseline all the in-scope elements on as-is basis. The idea is to hear the voice of the customer in their own words on organizational structure, business strategy, information technology, enterprise architecture, application portfolio, operational processes, infrastructure environment, governance models, and transformation imperatives.

Key Activities

Current Organization Assessment

In the current state assessment, the organization is assessed first to understand the roles and responsibilities within the organization, their decision-making styles, the strategic thinking of the executive, the role of business in IT, underlying governance mechanisms and measures, culture, the work ethic of the enterprise, and ability to embrace change. A primary source for assessment is published material like the organization's mission, vision, charter, structure, annual reports, job descriptions, skill profiles, and key performance indicators.

Illustrations for Organization Assessment

- In IT Strategy Consulting, organization assessment involves discussions with the CIO to understand the number of direct reports, distribution of business functions or IT portfolio, delineation of roles and responsibilities, the span of control, scope of operations, governance mechanisms, and monitoring functions like Office of CIO. In confidence, also get some insights into the professional/personal profile

---

18 Kancharla, M. (2016), *Consulting – A Practitioner's Perspective*, Notion Press.

Design Thinking in Current State Assessment   125

of key stakeholders. Collectively these inputs help classify stakeholders as influencers, decision makers, for or against the current initiative, or simply neutral.

- In IT Outsourcing Consulting, organization assessment is a four step process – 1] assessment of current organization structure taking into account the current roles, responsibilities, and governance mechanisms, 2] assessment of demand management process taking into account the role of business in defining projects scope, schedule and funding, the usage of these functionalities and their geographical spread, 3] assessment of organization manpower, parameters to be considered are the number of associates, nature of employment, role and skill profile and 4] assessment of the organizations experience in outsourcing and vendor management.

- In IT Governance Consulting, organization assessment involves understanding how decisions are made, what committees exist – their charter composition and frequency of cadence, how is the business value generated – being an efficient operator or solution integrator or innovation enabler, what are the governance processes at the enterprise level, at the functional level, how is the performance measured – translation of business goals to IT goals, metrics to measure achievement.

CURRENT BUSINESS ASSESSMENT

In the current state assessment, the business assessment would encompass baselining, management, and control – components that enable both management of the business and its control [examples are risk management and finance], business operations – components that handle the core business functions [examples are savings accounts in banks, merchandising in retail] and enabling services – components that have the functionality that is shared or common [examples are human resources, quality assurance, knowledge management]. Primary sources of information are corporate strategy developed at a group level and authorized by the board and business strategy documents developed by CEOs in alignment with the corporate strategy.

ILLUSTRATIONS FOR BUSINESS ASSESSMENT

- In IT Strategy Consulting, study the business strategy to understand the organization's vision, mission, values, strategic directions, revenue projections, growth targets, product/pricing strategies, market entry/exit strategies, customer acquisition strategies, competitive landscape, and measures for internal operational efficiencies covering people, process and technology. Next, translate strategy into action, by identifying strategic initiatives that are required to translate the vision into a reality, prioritize and detail with a well-defined scope, structure, stakeholders, schedule, and systems for management and monitoring. Additionally, interview business owners to get an overview of their function, goals, challenges, and opportunities for improvement. More importantly, their perspective on the current initiative, their requirements, and expectation from IT.

- In IT Architecture Consulting, to baseline the current business architecture, first identify the business components in the enterprise as this would localize the impact due to changes in the business environment and assist with decisions relating to the reuse of business components across units that have similar business processes. Once business components are identified, the next step is to group them into virtual layers based on operation domains to get a complete picture of the business architecture. This also enables a focus on business changes from an IT perspective.

- In IT Portfolio Management, parameters to be considered to baseline the business functionality are strategic alignment, business value, and risks. Strategic alignment is a combination of alignment to business strategy, alignment to IT strategy, and alignment to enterprise architecture. Business value is computed taking into account business criticality, breadth of use, usage profile, application life-cycle, business owner satisfaction, end user satisfaction, indicative datapoint number of business functions supported, geographic spread of users. Risks to be cataloged and mitigated are business impact risk, support risk, the risk to service level agreements, licensing risk, vendor risk and technical risk, indicative datapoint exposure to the organization if an application becomes unavailable.

- In IT Transformation Consulting, the assessment would span across the segments of the spectrum relevant for the transformation imperatives. Additionally, organizational impact assessment is conducted at a high level to understand structure, roles, responsibilities, skills, capabilities, culture, and behavior. The above results can be leveraged to create a change management strategy highlighting change interventions and their impact on transformation imperatives. Risks are then identified for the transformation imperatives and documented in a risk register, which is maintained and monitored through the transformation journey. Insights from these assessments, help refine the transformation charter.

CURRENT TECHNOLOGY ASSESSMENT

In the current state assessment, technology assessment would include evaluation of software applications, service delivery processes, and supporting infrastructure. Parameters to be considered to baseline the technology environment are technical value and operational health. Technical value is a measure of agility and alignment, indicated in terms of technology stack and architecture, lifecycle, and scalability of application [examples are the ability to support additional lines of business segments or products, application configuration, and personalization]. Operational health is a measure of performance, computed based on complexity, incident management, system responsiveness, and actual resolution time [examples are frequency of business changes, the volume of change requests]. Primary sources of information, interviews with CIO for strategic directions, application profiles for services provided, and maintenance history for operational data.

ILLUSTRATIONS FOR TECHNOLOGY ASSESSMENT

- In IT Strategy Consulting, technology assessment would mean mapping the applications to the business components they support in a structure similar to the business architecture and document the characteristics in terms of business criticality, functional fit, and flexibility to adapt to business change, platform diversity, future readiness, vendor interface, developmental plans, maintenance history, and open issues. Next understand how the business architecture is translated into application architecture, showing the linkages between the business functions and IT applications. Next map the information to the application components that support the business, in a structure similar to the application architecture, highlighting the directions of data-flow and attributes of data shared between applications. Lastly, map the infrastructure to the application and information components required to support the business.

- In IT Architecture Consulting for technology assessment, first baseline the current application architecture – helps in understanding the relations between applications, relations between applications and external agencies, in defining the framework of information and technology architecture components that need to be implemented to support the identified application functions. Next baseline the information architecture, which is a discipline for organizing and classifying information across enterprise, organization, and application boundaries so that it can be used effectively by the business. Lastly baseline the infrastructure architecture, which is a combination of system services, enabling functions provided by the operating systems, platform services, logical computer processing elements needed to support the execution of the business application, and network communication services.

- In IT Infrastructure Consulting, technology assessment would mean baselining inventory details of servers, storage, middleware, network, help desk, and data center. To understand what it takes to run the operations, a variety of additional parameters for each infrastructure component needs to be captured for subsequent analysis. For servers, the utilization is measured as a percentage of CPU utilization over a period of time, usually a year. For storage, the utilization is measured in terms of total available storage vs. used storage. Additionally, to understand how much it costs to run the operations, spend on IT infrastructure is calculated individually for all infrastructure components and classified as capital expenditure [CapEx] the upfront cost incurred by the physical equipment including the essential software to make it usable, and operational expenditure [OpEx] like maintenance fees, people expenses, external services costs, etc. Utilization data, spend data and the component specific parameters listed above provide meaningful insights into defining the potential for infrastructure optimization.

CURRENT PROCESSES ASSESSMENT

In the current state assessment, process assessment would encompass baselining the business processes to understand the workflow, points of manual intervention, steps that are automated, functions and resources touched upon by the processes, interfaces to external processes, and opportunities for improvement. Similarly, baseline the current IT processes, availability of standards, and compliance to the same along with an understanding of the reasons for deviation, if any, plus potential for optimization.

ILLUSTRATIONS FOR PROCESS ASSESSMENT

- In IT Process Consulting, process assessment could mean determining process improvement initiatives using best practice frameworks like CMMi. First identify the organizational area for appraisal, select the process areas for which objective evidence needs to be collected for analysis. Study the organization structure and select projects; picking mature or closed projects, different sizes, varying monetary value, executed in an onsite/offshore model and includes external IT service providers. The methods of examining objective evidence are document reviews and interviews. Documents considered for review are policy documents, standards and guidelines, project plans, estimation worksheets, process improvement plans, process deployment plans, training plans, and trackers for deployment/compliance. Interviews are also conducted to ascertain first-hand. how work is performed and managed, finding areas of strengths, weaknesses, and organizational issues.

- In IT Process Consulting, process assessment could also mean determining the potential for optimization using best practices frameworks like Lean. The starting point is a series of lean workshops to understand the voice of the customer, business, process and to capture high level value streams, pain points, and lean metrics. Lean principles addressed are specifying value by listing the services to be provided to the customer based on past data. Classify services into those that are critical and have a high impact, those that consume most of the effort, and those that the respective service executive would like to have assessed. Identifying value stream is a key concept used to deliver process optimization; it is a visual representation of the sequential flow of process activities, starts and ends with a customer, providing a systematic end-to-end view of the current environment, performance, and potential for optimization.

CURRENT GOVERNANCE ASSESSMENT

In current state assessment, governance assessment would mean baselining the current organization structure, roles, responsibilities, accountabilities, the span of control, sphere of influence, understanding the prevalent governance arrangements, mechanisms, processes, and measurements.

ILLUSTRATIONS FOR GOVERNANCE ASSESSMENT

- Governance Structure – In assessing the current governance structure, the emphasis is on the current IT organization. Interview all key stakeholders to understand their individual roles, responsibilities, reporting lines [at least one level above and one level below], goals, objectives, personal motivations, and key success criteria. Assess the existing committees as to who the chair is, what their charter is, what is the composition, and the frequency of their cadence. Obtain individual insights on how they perceive the target organization to be, in light of the current drivers being addressed.

- Governance Mechanisms – Assess how decisions are taken [i.e.] the closest archetype with regard to IT principles, IT architecture, IT infrastructure, business application needs, and IT investments. On investments, drill-down further on the distribution to infrastructure, transactional, informational, and strategic asset classes. Understand the modus operandi of their operating model, what is their approach to generating business value. By being an efficient operator or solution integrator or innovation enabler, cross check this position with their preference for centralization, additionally the effectiveness of IT governance in these models.

- Governance Processes – In assessing current governance processes, start with the enterprise level processes; these are a combination of key processes and enabling processes. Next, assess the processes at the function level across the governance layers. Critical to observe are the conformance and cross-linkages. Assess the maturity of governance processes on factors like awareness and communication, policies standards and procedures, tools and automation, skills and expertise, responsibility/accountability, and goal setting and measurement. Classify the maturity of each process as non-existent, initial, repeatable, defined, managed, or optimized.

Governance Measurements – Similar to processes, measures are also cascaded from the business goals to IT goals to process goals to activity goals. Current state assessment of governance measurements involves assessing the alignment of goals bottom-up and the defined metrics to measure achievement. Key metrics are cost effective use of IT, effective use of IT for growth, effective use of IT for asset utilization, and effective use of IT for business flexibility.

OUTCOMES

The outcome of this phase is the first interim deliverable, the current state assessment report. The baseline data is assessed to arrive at high-level observations on organizational structure, business strategy, information technology, enterprise architecture, application portfolio, operational processes, infrastructure environment, governance models, and transformation imperatives.

OPPORTUNITY FOR DESIGN THINKING

In the current state assessment, even though the set objective is to hear the voice of the customer in the first person, in conventional approach most of the information baselined is built on recorded data from documents or systems, which at best is third person view of the current state. Design thinking principles and practices provide opportunities to bring back the customer to the forefront and capture the real deal behind the raw data – the strategic thinking/directions and leadership potential to drive change in case of organization assessment, the degree of alignment between business and IT in business assessment, the capability of systems to support business changes in technology assessment, the operational challenges that can be factored into the current transformation in process assessment and the organizational dynamics reading between the lines of an organization chart in case of governance assessment.

Design Thinking in Current State Assessment

The Algorithm for Current State Assessment is built on the Design Thinking Principles of Embrace Ambiguity & Diversity and Openness to Radical Collaboration.

Embrace Ambiguity & Diversity

In the current state assessment, ambiguity could stem from the way in which the context or drivers are interpreted or from challenges in identifying potential sources of information and the data they may divulge. One way to address this dilemma is to embrace ambiguity by accepting the dichotomy and reaching out to a diverse set of stakeholders to address all possible angles for the task at hand through tactful maneuvering.

Design thinking practices that are related to embracing ambiguity & diversity and are required for the current state assessment are Interviewing Techniques and Journey Mapping.

Interviewing Techniques

Current state assessment is all about connecting with the stakeholders and the most effective form is through direct interviews. It allows to capture the voice of the customer, probe further to understand the real reasons behind the immediate response and make inferences based on keeping an eye on body language. The onus is on the interviewer to not only listen attentively but also to take notes diligently. Both expert interviews and group interviews can be leveraged in this phase.

1. Instantiation of Interviewing Techniques for IT Governance Consulting

    In IT Governance Consulting, the current state assessment is on the organization's governance structures, mechanisms, and processes. The

Design Thinking in Current State Assessment

Table 7-1: Design Grid for Current State Assessment

	Human-centered Design	Embrace Ambiguity & Diversity	Openness to Radical Collaboration	Co-Create Impactful Solutions	Implement & Iteratively Improvise
Empathy Maps	■				
User Personas	■	■			■
How Might We			■		
Storyboarding	■		■		
Interviewing Techniques		▲			
Brainstorming			▲		
Business Model Canvas			▲		
Journey Maps		▲			■
Affinity Diagrams			■	■	
Raskar's Hexagon		■			
Morphological Analysis				■	
Value Proposition Canvas	■				

interviewees are typically from the management layer and to some extent personnel from human resources, thus the technique applied here is expert interviews.

The interviewer, therefore, has to be experienced in engaging with executives to make the best use of their limited time, to be seen as trustworthy as considerable confidential information may be shared, to be able to cite trends from research and what worked or did not work based on past experience. Such characteristics will demonstrate personal equity and will mean executives extending the time allotted resulting in additional insights.

In addition to the above competencies and characteristics stated, interviewing techniques as a design thinking practice brings in a focus on empathy, allowing executives to overcome inhibitions and share insights on what is faltering where and with whom.

2. INSTANTIATION OF INTERVIEWING TECHNIQUES FOR IT OUTSOURCING CONSULTING

In IT Outsourcing Consulting, consider a scenario where the scope of work is around setting up a Vendor Management Office [VMO]. Different parts of the IT organization may be operating with different vendors and would have built up strong relationships because of which multiple vendors may be existing with similar services, with different contracts and service level agreements. The technique best suited here is group interviews.

The interviewer has to be more of a facilitator of the group; to be able to bring relationship managers out of their comfort zone and open them up to hear of experiences of other managers, services of other vendors, and be able to break from the bond of legacy agreements. Current state assessment in this context involves cataloging vendors, services provided, rate cards, and service level agreements in such a way that relationship managers can compare and contract efficiently and the organization as a whole can consolidate.

Conventional consulting would embark on just the above exercise, but by applying the design thinking principle of embracing diversity organizations can reach out to vendors too for group interviews. How many times do organizations get to know of other beta services of vendors and that too on a competitive yet collaborative platform?

Choosing the right interview technique and the right interviewer is critical for extracting meaningful insights from the stakeholders. Many a time, there will be information overload causing the right interpretation to escape. Here comes the equally important closing element of taking notes in real-time, sharing minutes within a 24-hour window and forcing feedback at the earliest.

JOURNEY MAPS

A journey map is the visualization of the steps an actor goes through in order to accomplish a particular goal. Once the generic path of the current state is established, it can be further tweaked to represent different personas. Each step in the journey map is marked with a series of actions, thoughts, emotions the actor goes through. Each step also depicts touchpoints, physical or virtual interaction with the product, service, or organization. Peg a timeline to the steps to make the journey complete.

1. INSTANTIATION OF JOURNEY MAPS FOR IT PROCESS CONSULTING

   IT Process Consulting largely deals with the optimization of processes and relies heavily on visual representations like workflow diagrams, swim-lane diagrams, etc. Journey maps are similar in nature, with additional focus on the user experience at each step.

   Consider a scenario of a Car Rental Agency wanting to simplify its rental process leveraging digital technologies to reduce the number of touchpoints, and be ready to capitalize on evolving digital channels. This requires an understanding of the steps the customer goes through to book a car and associated IT processes to know what applications to open, at what process step to open, and which partners to open to. Therefore, the suitability of journey maps not only plots the workflow but also the user interactions including timelines.

   The journey map starts with the 'Scenario' in this case, 'a potential customer trying to rent a car', then identify the 'Actor' in the scenario, here it's the 'potential customer'. Now list the 'Actions' the potential customer would go through to rent a car – 'find car rentals, compare offers, check insurance, reserve the best offer, review for upgrades, collect car keys, find out the parking lot, etc.'. For every action on the journey, capture – customers' experiences and emotions. Wherever the customer struggles that experience is flagged as negative. Similarly, capture steps that are non-value adding and flag them as redundant. Also, explore possibilities to integrate steps for simplicity and speed. Journey maps enable for baselining such insights.

Journey maps are a powerful tool to understand user experience, offer tremendous insights into what all pains points, emotional highs/lows a customer has to go through for a particular service; these insights provide opportunities for improvement and optimization. Journey maps also help identify redundant, superfluous actions and serve as an effective tool to boost productivity and save cost.

OPENNESS TO RADICAL COLLABORATION

The relevance of radical collaboration to current state assessment is evident from the need for diverse perspectives of every data point, not just what is visible and apparent but also the cause and effect be it for people, process, and/or technology. The reach, therefore, has to be across the organization and beyond if needed to be, not just with known and named resources but with anyone across the enterprise's value chain who can interpret the cause or can influence the effect.

Design thinking practices that are related to openness for radical collaboration and required for current state assessment are Brainstorming and Business Model Canvas.

BRAINSTORMING

Information gathering is at the core of current state assessment through interactions with stakeholders, be it through interviews in real-time or relayed through responses to questionnaires. Leveraging the design thinking principle of radical collaboration, the practice of brainstorming can be applied to allow for a meaningful debate on the available baseline information, thereby infusing insight into the information rather than remaining as a static data-point.

Design Thinking in Current State Assessment 137

1. INSTANTIATION OF BRAINSTORMING FOR IT PORTFOLIO MANAGEMENT

    In IT Portfolio Management, application rationalization is the most common scope element. Individually each application owner can at best share information about their application scope, architecture, infrastructure, and operational parameters.

    Conventional consulting takes this approach to baseline the above information and analyze the data independently at a later point in time. Design thinking lays emphasis on collaboration and by leveraging practices like brainstorming the application owners can be brought together to collectively assess the current application portfolio looking for synergies and economies of scale.

    The role of the facilitator is key; all applications are assessed to see if they need to be retired or re-engineered, or replaced. The applications should need not be judged by size but by business criticality, the best suited option for a given application need not come from the respective application owner but can evolve from ideas from other application owners.

Brainstorming at this stage is not to analyze or recommend a direction but to provide additional insight derived from the collective wisdom of application owners. Such insights and comparative inputs and are not necessarily evident from within the application profile, they make the task of subsequent phases of target state definition, analysis & findings easier.

BUSINESS MODEL CANVAS

Business model canvas is a visual chart that captures the nine key building blocks of a business model [i.e.] customer segments, value proposition, channels, customer relationships, revenue stream, key resources, key activities, key partnerships, and cost structure, all of which can be leveraged to understand the current state of the company and how the building blocks are currently collaborating to create value.

1. INSTANTIATION OF BUSINESS MODEL CANVAS FOR IT TRANSFORMATION CONSULTING

    In IT Transformation Consulting, the current state of all the five perspectives – organization, business, technology, process, and governance need to be assessed. Consider a scenario, wherein an IT organization is embarking on an internal digital transformation initiative to streamline its operations to support anytime/anywhere availability of their applications to their associates on any-device.

The assessment, therefore, needs to cover the breadth of the enterprise and the depth or degree of readiness on the five perspectives required to baseline the current state. The business model canvas can be leveraged to address both these objectives. First a given, the nine building blocks cover the breadth of the enterprise. Second, map elements of the five perspectives relevant to the transformation initiative to the respective building blocks. Third, assess the depth or degree of readiness for each of these elements.

Customer Segments, in a typical IT organization the segments would include development teams, solution architects, industry experts, sales representatives, and management executives. In a transformation initiative, it is important to baseline the requirements as serviced today, specifications for the planned transformation initiative, and any unmet needs along with their technical feasibility/business viability. Assess how development teams are taking care of project management today, how solution architects are able to collaborate and cross-leverage assets, how sales representatives are tracking their opportunity pipeline, managing their revenues, and how management is measuring and monitoring performance.

Value Proposition is anytime/anywhere availability of application on any device. And to achieve this transformation goal, it is important to baseline the platforms supported – desktops vs laptops, underlying environment – on premise mainframes vs on cloud web-based applications and the associated operational metrics – availability vs access of applications, periodic vs real-time reporting on performance.

Channels, the goal is to move to a web-based environment and be device agnostic. Therefore, the assessment needs to cover feasibility for migration, portability and through that the possibility for re-engineering or rationalization to enhance operational efficiencies. Equally important is to retire applications that fail to comply or contribute to this criterion.

Design Thinking in Current State Assessment

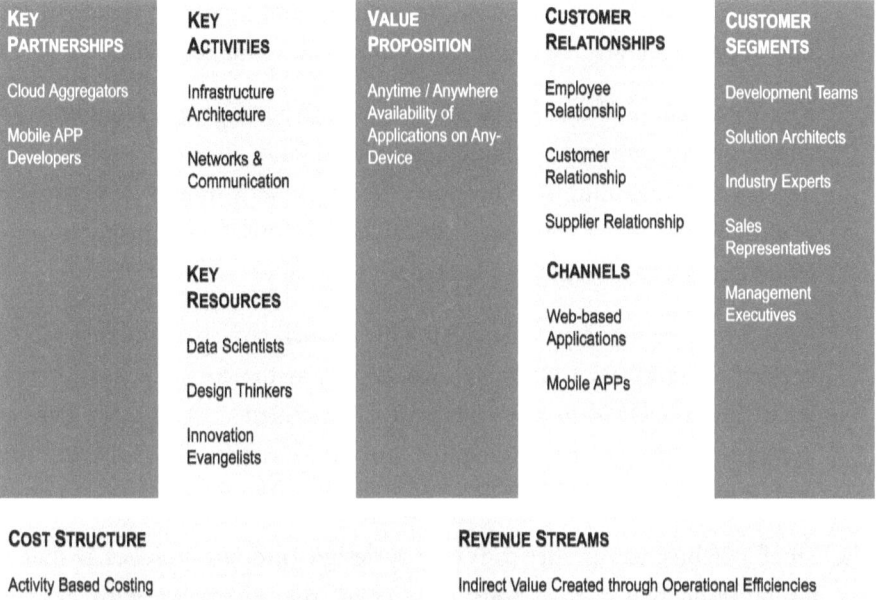

Figure 7-1: Business Model Canvas

Customer Relationships, this being an internal initiative, all the stakeholders are internal associates. The assessment covers existing communication protocols, reporting mechanisms, governance processes to establish current relationships and evaluate sustenance of the same in a digital world.

Revenue Stream is the indirect value created through operational efficiencies and to measure the same, first baseline current operational performance indicators such as system availability, response times, capacity utilization, concurrent users, information exchange between applications.

Key Resources, IT being a people intensive enterprise, resources are a given, but what really matters here is the skills and competencies of these resources – what is the availability of resources skilled in new technologies needed in a digital enterprise. Availability of manpower with creative skills like design thinking is a bonus.

Key Activities, to achieve the goal of availability of applications anywhere and any-device, the infrastructure backbone needs to be robust. Assess current configurations of systems, networks, communication protocols and how they are architected together to support real-time response.

Key Partnerships, in a digital enterprise, partnerships are required with cloud service providers, cloud aggregators, and also the mobile APP development community. Therefore, the assessment should cover current environments, access controls, security mechanisms, feasibility to move to cloud environments, mobile platforms.

Cost Structure, activity-based costing is one such cost structure that can be applied to an internal initiative such as this, as the costs are also internal to be absorbed within the enterprise. Assessment should cover current application span, usage, availability, and business criticality for each unit within the enterprise.

The benefit of business model canvas as a design thinking practice is that it lays out building blocks that holistically cover the enterprise, with defined characteristics at a component level and derived characteristics for cross-component collaboration. The canvas, therefore, is very comprehensive not just to paint the current state, but also to plot the target state.

Outcomes of Design Thinking

The instantiations above amply demonstrate how the principles and practices of design thinking can add value and provide additional insights. Even in a simple technique like interviewing, the focus shifts from gathering information mechanically to having an empathetic dialogue, allowing stakeholders to overcome inhibitions and openly share experiences. Business processes are plotted as journey maps to discover any unmet needs. Collaboration amongst application owners and third-party service providers is encouraged to explore synergies and economies of scale. The differentiator of design thinking lies in how the assessment is extended to adjacent entities of the enterprise, more importantly how the assessment itself is conducted.

Key Learnings

In the current state assessment, the coverage is on the organizational, business, technology, process, and governance perspectives of the enterprise. The assessment relies on responses from stakeholders through interviews and on the study of existing documentation. Conventionally the objective of this state is to just baseline and document the current state.

The organization is first assessed to the strategic thinking of the executive, competitive position of the enterprise, and business drivers and directions, the primary source in published material in the public domain. In business assessment, the role of business in IT is assessed, primary sources of information are corporate, business, and IT strategy documents. Technology assessment includes software applications, enterprise architecture, and infrastructure, primary sources of information are application profiles, architecture diagrams, and operational data. Process assessment would encompass baselining business processes and associated IT processes, primary sources of information are workflow diagrams. In governance assessment, organization structure, roles, responsibilities, governance arrangements, mechanisms, and processes are baselined; the primary source of information is interviews with executives.

Design thinking principles and practices provide opportunities to bring back the customer to the forefront and capture the real deal behind the raw data and infuse insight into the information gathered. Principles relevant to current state assessment are Embracing ambiguity and diversity and Openness to radical collaboration. Embracing ambiguity advocates ambiguity by accepting the dichotomy and reaching out to a diverse set of stakeholders to address all possible angles for the ask. Openness to radical collaboration encourages reach across the organization and beyond if need be, not just with known and named resources but with anyone across the enterprise value chain who can interpret the cause or can influence the effect.

Practices related to embracing ambiguity and diversity are Interviewing and Journey maps. Interviewing techniques are of two types – Expert interviews and Group interviews. The onus is on the interviewer to capture the voice of the customer, probe further to understand the real reasons behind the immediate response, which requires attentive listening and diligent taking of notes. In journey maps, the goal is not just mapping the generic path but understanding the emotions and actions at every step that the actor goes through.

Practices related to openness to radical collaboration are Brainstorming and Business model canvas. Brainstorming is conventionally applied during solutioning, but design thinking encourages application during current state assessment also as it values collective wisdom ideated by all stakeholders concerned. Business model canvas is a visual representation of the big-picture of the current state across the breadth of the enterprise including depth which is the organization's degree of readiness.

The above four practices have been applied to illustrative activities across the consulting spectrum. The instantiations demonstrate the relevance of design thinking, by highlighting the importance of empathy in interviewing, embracing diversity to get a wider perspective of the current state, understanding of user experiences, and the value of collective wisdom gained through collaboration.

. Ω .

Chapter 8

Design Thinking in Target State Definition

In Target State Definition, the objective is to realize the to-be environment that addresses the challenges of the context and current state of the enterprise. The definition should include some or all of the following; organizational changes required in light of the concern being addressed, its potential position vis-à-vis the market/competition, the business in terms of the products and/or services the organization offers enhancements to technology and infrastructure that supports the business, the processes that the organization operates with, re-alignment of the structures and mechanisms that the organization is governed by, and last but not the least the people and cultural adjustments needed for the new organization. Note, in defining the target state inline with these elements, it is equally important to ensure adherence to external elements like industry regulations and alignment to market dynamics of the changing environment.

Design Thinking is amply suited to define the target state as it acknowledges the challenges of the current state; based on which it explores alternatives to address the context in a collaborative manner. Characteristics of design thinking that can complement the target state are; definitions derived through convergent insights. The ideation is cumulative, incrementally building on each idea without rejecting any, inclusivity in keeping end customers in-mind and addressing their unmet needs even of the extreme users.

In this chapter, Design Thinking as applied to the Target State Definition phase of consulting is explained, starting with an overview of the consulting phase with illustrations for activities across consulting segments, leading to the customization of the Design Grid by selecting relevant Principles and related Practices. These intersections are further detailed as to how they can enhance target state definition, including instantiations for select segments of the consulting spectrum.

Target State Definition

Objectives

The objective of the Target State Definition[19] phase is to define the target state of all the in-scope elements on a to-be basis. The idea is to hear the aspirations of the customer, on organizational structure, business strategy, information technology, enterprise architecture, application portfolio, operational processes, infrastructure environment, governance models, and transformation imperatives.

Key Activities

Target Organization Definition

In target state definition, the organization is re-defined in terms of its structure, resources, and capabilities. Questions to be addressed are - How should the organization be restructured to support the redefined business model, functions, and/or processes? What should be the size of the resource pool? How should these resources be distributed? What skills and competencies should the resources master to service the enhanced technology platform? The target audience to evaluate the above should be limited and left to the discretion of the executive sponsor. Ideally, a small forum of one or two business and IT representatives participating under the supervision of the sponsor should suffice. Note, some of the discussions may happen sans consultants because of organizational sensitivities.

Illustrations for Organization Definition

- In IT Strategy Consulting, target organization definition involves discussions with CIO to define the structure of the organization – centralized vs de-centralized, decision making styles – authoritative vs collaborative, roles and responsibilities, job descriptions, competency

---

19 Kancharla, M. (2016), *Consulting – A Practitioner's Perspective*, Notion Press.

- profiles, matchmaking of executives to entities, establishing span of control and span of influence and most importantly, sensing the organizational readiness to change.

- In IT Outsourcing Consulting, the target operating model definition involves re-drawing the organization, the structure of the outsourced organization, the structure of the retained organization, and the interfacing entities between the two structures. And for target resource model involves the definition of resource requirements both in capacity and capability terms – how much needs to be sourced based on how much is available in-house, how many need to be at onsite, how many at offshore, how should the knowledge transfer and transition take place.

- In IT Governance Consulting, target IT functions are designed so as to reinforce the business imperatives that define the strategic performance of a firm based on end customer needs. Very soon the role of a Business Relationship Manager will emerge as a key role. The relationship manager acts as an interface between business and IT; helps business units by identifying solutions, and helps IT by becoming an advocate of technology in business. Additional factors considered are market dynamics, industry trends, customer needs, competitor moves, organizational culture, internal strategic directions like organizational growth, and geographic spread.

Target Business Definition

In target state definition, business definition revolves around qualifying strategic initiatives and quantifying strategic directions. How to achieve the set growth targets? What products can best deliver these results and at what price? What business functions are impacted? How do we optimize the underlying business processes and build synergies? The above questions are best resolved in a cross-functional workshop, brainstorming with the respective business heads and the executive sponsor to debate and decide on the target definitions.

Illustrations for Business Definition

- In IT Strategy Consulting, target business strategy starts with the identification of improvement initiatives, parameters for prioritization, measures, and means to achieve targets and their impact on the enterprise, exposure to risk, management, and mitigation of the same. Improvement initiatives could be products that need to be launched, markets to be expanded, the alliance to be forged to foray into new geographies or operational efficiencies required in business processes, effective utilization of resources or automation of manual activities, and the need for integrated and consistent service delivery. And in doing so, foster a culture of knowledge creation, collaboration, and consumption

- In IT Architecture Consulting, target business architecture needs to answer the following questions – how the organization plans to accomplish its mission and what is the model for communicating the business to the various stakeholders across the enterprise. In defining the business architecture, revisit the business vision, objectives, and strategies, the IT vision, objectives, and strategies through the study of existing architecture blueprints in conjunction with new and emerging technologies. Prioritize the strategic directions of the enterprise is it cost reduction, operational efficiency, or the economies of scale to enhance profit realization. The key is to accomplish this task through joint planning with all stakeholders for collective buy-in and sustainability, bear in mind getting the business architecture right is extremely critical as the rest of the architecture components are derived from these first principles.

- In IT Portfolio Management, the target business functionality is determined by each application's strategic and business value, how they are rated today, and their future growth potential. In general, high value rated applications is important to the business today and tomorrow. It will most likely be a candidate in the target solution. On the other hand, low value rated applications are of no or limited use to the business and need to be considered for retirement as a prioritized option. Medium rated applications need to be further investigated and could be frozen temporarily.

- In IT Transformation Consulting, the definition would span across the segments of the spectrum relevant for the transformation imperatives. Additionally, change agents who can help deliver the business change are identified by promoting the case for change amongst peers and colleagues, enabling people to work effectively as they plan, implement and experience change and increasing people's ability to manage future change. Risks are evaluated to determine the potential impact and probability of occurrence in the transformation program. Results are leveraged to prioritize risks and define mitigation strategies. Transformation management office with responsibilities for developing the master plan for transformation, stakeholder management, financial management, and communications management is established.

TARGET TECHNOLOGY DEFINITION

In target technology definition, the debate shifts to the identified IT imperatives, what should be its scope, span of control, the span of impact, business dependencies, and their future proof quotient. Target technology is a function of an application, information, and technical architectures. The application architecture needs to determine, how aligned the application components are to the business components and what is the quality of services being provided to the business. The information architecture needs to determine, what data components are required by the application components, how the data is to be structured, and what is the level of integration required for optimal usage of information. The technical architecture needs to determine, what infrastructure components are required by the application/information components, what is required configuration for operational efficiency, and how is the quality of service to be defined. All the above questions require a healthy debate between the business and the IT, chaired by the executive sponsor and moderated by the consultant. The expectation is to arrive at a consensus solution that is co-created through collaboration; a technology platform that meets the needs of the business with a promise of operational efficiencies.

ILLUSTRATIONS FOR TECHNOLOGY DEFINITION

- In IT Strategy Consulting, technology definition would mean establishing linkages between IT imperatives and business imperatives, prioritizing IT projects as per their contribution to new business strategies, optimizing IT investment distribution and spend patterns to yield higher returns on investment. This would require, discovering innovative technologies, instituting a flexible enterprise architecture, a secure infrastructure that is efficiently utilized with defined service level agreements. In essence, the target state should become an enabler for competitive advantage

- In IT Architecture Consulting for technology definition, the application architecture first needs to be defined by logically grouping the target business processes as per the business architecture into application components. Focus is on functional coverage of current applications. Secondly, define the information architecture, by revisiting the guidelines for the use and deployment of all information resources and assets across the enterprise. Focus is on information blueprints that maximizes value, use, and security of information assets. Lastly define the technical architecture, comprises data centers, domain platforms, delivery channels, security gateways/firewalls, and systems management. Focus is on resilient and reliable infrastructure with minimal redundancy

- In IT Infrastructure Consulting, technology definition would mean identification of infrastructure components that have pockets of underutilization and evaluate ways to increase the same to optimum levels. In defining the target infrastructure, parameters to keep in mind are scalability, manageability, simplicity, stability, reliability, availability, agility, and flexibility. And for optimizing infrastructure, explore virtualization of infrastructure to boost utilization at all levels. Though there may be an upfront cost for virtualization, its benefits outperform the investment. Additionally, evaluate managed service models or hosted infrastructure that takes away CAPEX cost and includes OPEX expenses only.

Target Processes Assessment

In target state definition, process definition involves determining the most realistic and sustainable maturity level for the selected process areas. In case of process improvement, the target definition is pre-determined as part of the engagement objectives itself; in fact, the current state is assessed against these goals, leading to gap analysis directly. In process optimization initiatives, the target definition could be expressed as – the creation of a single standard process using best practice from

Design Thinking in Target State Definition 149

existing processes, by applying lean principles, focusing on select value streams to be workable on the target date resulting in achieving efficiency gains. Stakeholders involved in process definition are engagement sponsor, process leader, and process champions.

Illustrations for Process Definition

- In IT Process Consulting, for process improvement initiatives, the target state is defined as – 1]. Using CMMI as the improvement framework, appraise the process maturity of selected process areas against a certain capability level or appraise the process maturity of the organization against a certain maturity level, 2]. Using the findings of the appraisal develop an action plan for bridging the gaps and improving internal processes.

- In IT Process Consulting, for process optimization initiatives the steps followed are identifying the value add, non-value add, and operational value add process steps in the current value stream map. Value additions are something the customer would pay for, even if the payment is theoretical, the principle here is that the customer would see the activity as adding value to the output. Non-value additions are activities the customer would not pay for; it does not add value to the unit from their perspective. Operational value additions are activities the customer would not pay for, but are essential to ensure the process or the business can run smoothly, also referred to as enabling value additions. Subsequent steps are designing future state activity blocks, estimated performance and benefits, and developing future state value streams for select processes. Future state activity blocks are action items that need to be implemented to reach the desired future state of a value stream. Forces end-to-end thinking; breaking the system into manageable but related loops for implementation and quantifying improvement potential.

Target Governance Assessment

In target state definition, governance definition would mean designing the target organization structure. required roles at a functional level and committees at a group level along with associated responsibilities and accountabilities. Implicitly included are the governance mechanisms, processes, and measurements. Business leadership, IT leadership, chairpersons of strategy, planning, and governance committees need to be consulted by the engagement sponsor.

ILLUSTRATIONS FOR GOVERNANCE DEFINITION

- Governance Mechanisms – Define the orientation that would be best suited to achieve the business goals taking into account the capabilities and challenges of the current IT organization. The orientation will have a bearing on the governance mechanisms and governance arrangement. In profit-oriented firms, governance mechanisms should focus on seamless management incorporation of IT, tracking of business value by measuring and monitoring IT investments, and allocation of IT costs to business units. In growth-oriented firms, governance mechanisms should focus on selective decentralization, centralize corporate systems and infrastructure, decentralize business unit-specific application development, the emphasis is on resource management and integration

- Governance Processes – IT organizations are best designed around processes that deliver services to the business. In a workshop mode with IT leadership, shape the target governance processes, more importantly, get consensus and buy-in. For each of the IT functions across the governance, layers identify the business touchpoints and study the business process to effectively define the necessary governance processes, examples are project prioritization, project management, project development, quality assurance, and implementation processes, for each such process define an owner and the targeted maturity level. As the governance processes mature, IT becomes a better team-based organization, ready to assemble and deploy resources wherever and whenever business mandates.

- Governance Measurements – Key Goal Indicators [KGI's] and Key Performance Indicators [KPI's] are defined post defining the governance structure, mechanisms and processes. The Balanced Scorecard is a fit for purpose framework. KGIs tell whether a goal has been achieved or not after the fact, the focus is on customer and financial dimensions of the balanced scorecard, they are lag indicators. KPIs are a measure of how well the process is performing to predict the probability of success or failure in the future, focus is on the process and learning dimensions of the balanced scorecard, they are the lead indicators.

OUTCOMES

The outcome of this phase is the second interim deliverable, the target state definition report. The target definition should be feasible and sustainable with the buy-in of all stakeholders. Representation may vary from function to function, but at a minimum, the target state is defined in terms of the result of the change, rationale for change, rewards for action, and risk of in-action. The enterprise architecture should address both business and technology drivers. Business processes are improvised and optimized; the infrastructure environment should deliver operational efficiencies.

OPPORTUNITY FOR DESIGN THINKING

In target state definition, divergent thinking becomes the need of the hour, to envision what should be the characteristics of the future state that would not only solve the current problems but also be sustainable on its own. In a conventional approach, target state definition, in most cases is limited to finding answers to problems, while in design thinking, the approach is more of sensing the real problem and responding in a way that addresses all stakeholders, including end customers. Design thinking principles and practices provide opportunities for divergent stakeholders to come together to collaboratively define their future state in a way that everyone feels part of the solution and therefore the drive to make it succeed and sustain.

DESIGN THINKING IN TARGET STATE DEFINITION

The Algorithm for Target State Definition is built on the Design Thinking Principles of Embrace Ambiguity & Diversity and Openness to Radical Collaboration.

EMBRACE AMBIGUITY & DIVERSITY

In the target state definition, the focus is on the diversity aspect of this design thinking principle. Embrace diversity across all dimensions of the consulting

Table 8-1: Design Grid for Target State Definition

	Human-centered Design	Embrace Ambiguity & Diversity	Openness to Radical Collaboration	Co-Create Impactful Solutions	Implement & Iteratively Improvise
Empathy Maps	■				
User Personas	■	▲			■
How Might We			■		
Storyboarding	■		■		
Interviewing Techniques		■			
Brainstorming		■			
Business Model Canvas		▲			
Journey Maps		■			■
Affinity Diagrams			▲	■	
Raskar's Hexagon		■	▲		
Morphological Analysis				■	
Value Proposition Canvas	■				

continuum – people, process, and technology. In defining the future state, solutions can be found in close proximity purely as a fix to the immediate problem, such solutions may qualify to be a tick in the box, but are seldom sustainable. Therefore, the need for opening up the playing field to include all stakeholders, accounting for all possibilities be it in business, technology, infrastructure, regulation or culture and most importantly end customer point of view, the key here is balance.

Design thinking practices that are related to embracing ambiguity & diversity and required for target state definition are User Personas and Business Model Canvas.

User Personas

User personas help in building up the right profile that would best fit the future state. The profile here can be the executive who would run the transformed enterprise to achieve its new goals in the context of IT Strategy Consulting or IT Governance Consulting, or managers of the retained organization to manage the vendor management office in the context of IT Outsourcing Consulting.

1. **Instantiation of User Personas for IT Strategy Consulting**

    In IT Strategy Consulting, user personas can help in building up the profile of stakeholders and the skills they need to possess. Consider a scenario, wherein the enterprise is embarking on digital transformation for which they would also need to identify an executive sponsor.

    In order to accomplish the above goal, the conventional approach relies on studying existing competencies, identify enhancements required, and then select executives from the available management pool to lead the initiative.

    On the other hand, by leveraging the principles of design thinking principles to develop a persona, the focus is redirected to the future state and future customers, the profile thus created can truly drive the organization in its digital journey. The persona may also force CXOs to look beyond current organization structure, current roles, and executives performing these functions to establishing an independent function and a head to drive the digital transformation, say a Chief Digital Officer.

2. INSTANTIATION OF USER PERSONAS FOR IT GOVERNANCE CONSULTING

In IT Governance Consulting, user personas can help in structuring the various committees, factoring in individual roles, interpersonal relationships, and intra-committee collaboration required for the effective functioning of the committee.

In a conventional approach, only standard committees are constituted and amongst them, only those that are required for regulatory compliance are prioritized first. In composing the committee, in terms of deciding who the chair should be, hierarchy takes precedence. Post which, the member selection becomes the prerogative of the chair.

Important to note here is, user personas can be used not only for individuals but also for entities. A user persona can be drawn up for, say a 'Corporate Social Responsibility' committee. The principle allows for building up the profile of the committee and through that defining – 1] Governance principles – something beyond compliance, investing a certain percentage to picking up a real cause, say sustainability, 2] Governance structures – getting rid of the concept of a chair and embracing a federated structure or even better a round-table of experts in environment, alternative energy, 3] Governance measures – not to be confined by metrics that a balance sheet mandates, but by the real impact made to the society at large.

3. INSTANTIATION OF USER PERSONAS FOR IT OUTSOURCING CONSULTING

In IT Outsourcing Consulting, user personas come in handy to define the profile required for the future state, as there would be a major change in the role and responsibility of the application owners, with the core functionality shifting to the service provider.

In outsourcing analysis, the focus pre-dominantly is on the applications or infrastructure being outsourced, capabilities of the service provider to support and adhere to the service level agreements, without much attention to the existing application owners.

User personas can be used to redraw the profile of application owners, in light of their residual role and responsibilities by virtue of outsourcing and the additional responsibilities that also come with outsourcing [i.e.] vendor management. By drawing up the user personas with these implied changes of the future state, organizations can upfront re-evaluate current application owners if they are still best suited for the redrawn profile, if not they can plan for replacement and be ready for the transition.

The above instantiations amply demonstrate how the design thinking practice of user personas can aid in defining the future state and also in preparing for the same. More importantly, it facilitates exploring alternative perspectives – is there a need for new roles, establishing guidelines for the new role be it for an individual or a group, taking into consideration the revised responsibilities and through that the best profile is chosen and prepared for the persona.

BUSINESS MODEL CANVAS

Business model canvas is a visual chart that captures the nine key building blocks of a business model [i.e.] customer segments, value proposition, channels, customer relationships, revenue stream, key resources, key activities, key partnerships, and cost structure. Like in the current state assessment, all the building blocks are equally relevant for target state definition. The practice of business model canvas helps in envisioning, what should be the sphere of operations and span of control of each component and how they need to co-exist in the future state.

1. **INSTANTIATION OF BUSINESS MODEL CANVAS FOR IT TRANSFORMATION CONSULTING**

   In IT Transformation Consulting, the target state of all the five perspectives – organization, business, technology, process, and governance need to be defined. Extending the same scenario of current state assessment, wherein an IT organization is embarking on an internal digital transformation initiative to streamline its operations to support anytime/anywhere availability of their applications to their associates on any-device. The instantiation here focuses on the changes that the future state is likely to bring-in.

The definition, therefore, needs to cover the objectives of each component and the outcomes as expected of the future state across all the five perspectives. The business model canvas can be leveraged to address both these perspectives. First a given; as in the current state assessment, all the nine building blocks cover the breadth of the future enterprise. Second, define the scope of elements impacted across the five perspectives relevant to the transformation initiative. Third, define the expected outcomes for impacted elements in order to meet the transformation objectives.

Customer Segments, Development teams, solution architects, industry experts, sales representatives, and management executives, would still continue to exist as segments of an IT organization. However, in a digital world, the nature of work in the future state would necessitate changes in way of working moving from waterfall method of development to agile, migrating from on premise environment to cloud platforms, and siloed style of functioning to team-based collaboration. On the sales front, winning formulae shifts from independent bidding to partnerships, leveraging third party niche service providers and aggregators to remain competitive. In the case of management, regulatory requirements transition from compliance to data privacy and protection.

Value Proposition is anytime/anywhere availability of application on any device. Easier said than done, the challenge is not so much in arriving at the technical solution but in operationalizing the same. The organization's ability to change is key to success, internally with the employees, externally with clients, partners, competitors, and regulatory bodies. And to accomplish all of these, there is a dire need for a new customer segment 'Digital Champions', who would act as a bridge between the old and new and guide the transformation to not only succeed but to sustain.

Channels, in line with the value proposition, channels should transcend platforms and devices, ensuring that the transition is smooth and in real-

Design Thinking in Target State Definition

time. Needless to say, an assistant to help navigate would be a blessing, to be more precise a digital assistant. The answer lies in a new channel 'Chatbots', an interactive digital help window to explore and experience the enhanced functions of the future state.

Customer Relationships, though this is an internal initiative, unlike the current state assessment, post-transformation the target state may see new entities in the enterprise ecosystem. Communication protocols, reporting mechanisms, governance processes may remain the same, but the channels may change, and expected response times are much faster.

Revenue Stream is the indirect value created through operational efficiencies. Metrics to define, monitor and measure are response times on a device, response time to transfer from one device to another, and availability of applications across platforms. Last but not the least, in a digital world, it's the user experience that matters.

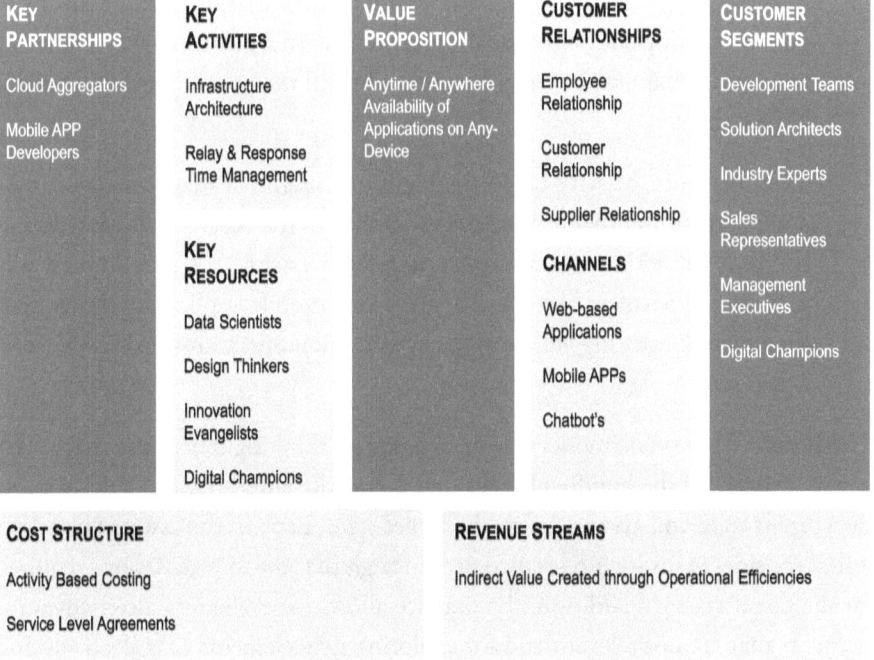

Figure 8-1: Business Model Canvas

Key Resources, IT being a people intensive enterprise, resources are a given, but what really matters here is the skills and competencies of these resources in emerging technologies like artificial intelligence, machine learning, data science, and creative skills like design thinking. The organization should patronize such competencies and promote such resources as digital champions.

Key Activities, to achieve the goal of availability of applications anywhere and any-device, the infrastructure backbone needs to be robust to meet the relay and response times of the target state. In a digital world, the robustness of the infrastructure architecture has a direct bearing on business performance, or to put it in the other way, the expected response time can be achieved only through the efficiency of the infrastructure.

Key Partnerships, in a digital enterprise, partnerships are required with cloud service providers, cloud aggregators, and also the mobile APP development community. Therefore, the definition should cover information exchange protocols, access controls, security mechanisms as part of the formal contractual agreements. And informally, a culture of trust and collaboration must be fostered, with the belief that it will benefit both parties.

Cost Structure, activity-based costing is one such cost structure that can be applied to an internal initiative such as this, as the costs are also internal to be absorbed within the enterprise to a large extent. And in a limited way with digital partners like cloud aggregators, mobile application developers, for which the costing will be as per agreed upon operations and service level agreements.

The benefit of business model canvas as a design thinking practice is that it lays out holistically all the building blocks that define the enterprise not only to assess the current state and also to define the target state. Each of the assessed elements is first considered for their relevance and through that the improvisations required for the target state. In addition, the practice allows for evaluating alternatives for elements that are not relevant and for exploring new elements to collectively and comprehensively achieve the target state.

Design Thinking in Target State Definition

OPENNESS TO RADICAL COLLABORATION

The relevance of radical collaboration to target state definition is evident from the need for convergence of diverse perspectives, not just what is visible and apparent but also for its impact, be it for people, process and/or technology. The reach, therefore, has to be across the organization and beyond if needed to be, not just with known and named resources but with anyone across the enterprise value chain who can influence the effect.

Design thinking practices that are related to openness to radical collaboration and required for target state definition are Affinity Diagrams and Raskar's Hexagon.

AFFINITY DIAGRAMS

Affinity diagrams are a key management tool for strategic planning. Leveraging the design thinking principle of radical collaboration, the practice of affinity diagram can be applied to generate, organize, and consolidate information concerning the target state of a product, a process, or any complex issue. This creative process fosters embracing diverse views and ideas without quantifying them but organizing them into groups or themes based on their relationships.

1. **INSTANTIATION OF AFFINITY DIAGRAMS FOR IT STRATEGY CONSULTING**

    In IT Strategy Consulting, the focus is on strategic initiatives around products, processes, services, structures, and systems that will shape the future state.

    In conventional consulting, in defining the target state, ideas are focused on set themes for the above five perspectives. Hence sometimes the consultants may feel constrained in generating ideas, would not be able to cross leverage across perspectives, and in the process, there is an inherent risk that some really good ideas may fall by the wayside.

    Design thinking on the other hand encourages ideation, to generate as many ideas as possible across perspectives, part of this gets done in the current state assessment, knowing where the organization is and visualizing options for the future. The information thus available is organized into themes/groups based on the relationships of the information. Post which, themes that resonate with the strategic objectives are taken forward to define the target state. Critical to the success of such working sessions is the role of the facilitator, how he or she navigates the group building upon ideas without discarding any, and in doing so, being true to the spirit of design thinking.

2. INSTANTIATION OF AFFINITY DIAGRAMS FOR IT GOVERNANCE CONSULTING

IT Governance Consulting, the focus is on governance structure, mechanisms, measures, and processes, that need to be put in place for the future organization to function in adherence to the defined strategic directions.

Conventional approaches to organization design, rely on industry patterns to define the governance styles to a large extent. Once the style is pegged, the process follows pre-defined governance guidelines and guardrails.

Design thinking principles when applied to organization design through practices like affinity diagrams, provide for an additional cover to ensure that the future organizational structure is sustainable. The basic usage of affinity diagrams continues to be grounded in ideation and grouping of ideas, the said addition is stakeholders' emotions and expectations; this added dimension to grouping would go a long way in governing the future organization.

3. INSTANTIATION OF AFFINITY DIAGRAMS FOR IT PORTFOLIO MANAGEMENT

In defining the target state for IT Portfolio Management, the focus is on the spending of the IT portfolio. Costs include hardware, software, infrastructure, licensing, project, and personnel costs and the challenge is in defining and balancing these elements.

Conventionally target portfolio definition relies on quantitative data, while these are rewarding inputs, the risk lies in overlooking paradigm-shifting insights. The information has the tendency to be concealed behind vague

Design Thinking in Target State Definition

observations or free form responses to traditional information gathering techniques. Here lies the limitation, the lack of study of qualitative data points, which bring to light the limitations, positive experiences, and end goals of key owners of the IT portfolio.

Affinity diagrams can give specific micro insights into what elements the team needs to focus on for target state definition. Affinity diagrams can be used to group and codify ideas, hypotheses, and predictions, focusing on appropriate application and understanding implications. Insights produced from affinity diagrams can be used to justify IT portfolio decisions, in ways that could move the needle from being acceptable to being exceptional.

The benefit of affinity diagrams as a design thinking practice is it encourages diverse views and ideas and without prejudice groups them based on the relationships of the information and, emotions and expectations of stakeholders. Themes thus evolved to help define the target state better aligned to the strategic objectives.

RASKARS HEXAGON

An enterprise that is open to radical collaboration, can effectively leverage the practice of Raskar's hexagon as it postulates building upon ideas from a given idea. In the context of the target state, many a time a solution may not sustain on its own and would require the supplemental elements also to be in-sync, and this exactly how the Raskar's hexagon is propagated. To re-iterate the caution flagged earlier, the starting idea or solution must be accurate.

1. **INSTANTIATION OF RASKAR'S HEXAGON FOR IT ARCHITECTURE CONSULTING**

    Enterprise architecture is a combination of business, application, technology, and infrastructure architectures. In most cases, the definition is top-down starting with business and ending with infrastructure. However, there could be scenarios like architecture definition for eCommerce, wherein the starting point is the infrastructure architecture.

Either way, in conventional consulting approaches, the focus is on defining the primary layer completely and then expanding upon the defined building blocks as relevant for the subsequent layers.

Leveraging the principle of radical collaboration in conjunction with Raskar's hexagon, enterprise architectures can be defined dynamically and in an agile manner. Ideate first on the primary layer and then build upon that idea for the other layers using any of the methods of Raskar's hexagon for arriving at new ideas.

Consider a scenario of developing an enterprise architecture for a new eCommerce business launch, the strategic objective for the enterprise is to reduce the response time to much less than existing benchmarks.

1. X^d the starting point can be to ideate on ways to define the business architecture to address a reduction in response time.

2. X+Y the contrasting idea and the combination that would make the primary idea interesting is to complement the business architecture directly to the infrastructure architecture.

3. X̄ in a way this is also the opposite of what would conventionally be done [i.e.] moving from business to application to technical architectures.

4. X↑ in ideating directly on the infrastructure architecture, the enterprise can also explore third party aggregators who have niche solutions to precisely such problems.

5. X↓ once the infrastructure architecture is conceptualized, revisit application and technology architectures can further be synchronized to address the core business proposition.

6. X++ Add an adjective to the idea, 'Architecture @ the speed of click'.

The benefit of Raskar's hexagon as a design thinking practice is it helps ideate on a core idea and guide in extrapolating corollary ideas, be it complementary, combinatory or contrasting. Raskar's hexagon aids in finding every possible problem that the idea can solve and also finding every possible solution to the problem, thus enabling a comprehensive definition of the target state.

OUTCOMES OF DESIGN THINKING

The instantiations above amply demonstrate how the principles and practices of design thinking aid in articulating adjacent and alternative definitions for the target state. Practices like user personas help in visualizing the profile required for the future. The profile here is not limited to just the person but can also be extended to entities, making adjustments as necessary and most importantly making stakeholders aware and be prepared. The same approach can be applied to external elements of the enterprise like customer segments, customer relationships, partnerships, channels, cost structures, and revenue streams to ensure that the value proposition is complete and comprehensive.

KEY LEARNINGS

In target state definition, the focus is on the to-be environment that addresses the challenges of the context and current state of the enterprise. The definition is built based on the aspirations of the customer – organizational structure, business strategy, information technology, enterprise architecture, application portfolio, operational processes, infrastructure environment, governance models, and transformation imperatives.

An organization is defined in terms of its structure, resources, and capabilities. Business definition revolves around qualifying strategic initiatives and quantifying strategic directions. Technology definition, the debate shifts to the identified IT imperatives. Process definition involves determining the most realistic and sustainable maturity level for the selected process areas. Governance definition would mean designing the target organization structure and required roles/responsibilities.

Design thinking principles and practices provide opportunities for divergent stakeholders to come together to collaboratively define their future state in a way that everyone feels part of the solution and therefore the drive to make it succeed and sustain.

Principles relevant to target state definition are Embrace Ambiguity & Diversity and Openness to Radical Collaboration. In the target state definition, the focus is on the diversity aspect of the first principle and the second principle is relevant for convergence of diverse perspectives.

Practices related to embracing ambiguity and diversity User Personas and Business Model Canvas. User personas help in building up the right profile that would best fit the future state. Business model canvass helps in envisioning the target state's sphere of operations and span of control.

Practices related to openness to radical collaboration are Affinity Diagrams and Raskar's Hexagon. Affinity diagrams are applied to generate, organize, and consolidate information concerning the target state. Raskar's hexagon helps in building corollary ideas from a given core idea.

The above four practices have been applied to illustrative activities across the consulting spectrum; the instantiations demonstrate the relevance of design thinking by highlighting the importance of holistically defining all building blocks at an enterprise level and creating the right profile at an individual level. Information from the current state assessment is aggregated with insights from ideating and without prejudice grouping taking into consideration the emotions/ expectations of stakeholders. Initiatives thus evolved will help in defining a target state aligned to strategic objectives.

. Ω .

Chapter 9

Design Thinking in Analysis and Findings

In Analysis & Findings phase, the focus is on studying gaps between the current state and future state and analysis of findings in order to arrive at recommendations. An analysis is carried out across the business, technology, and organization dimensions, individually and collectively. The business analysis comprises a static assessment of the business based on parameters like policy, product, price, projections, and performance in terms of how they currently stack up and the degree of development required for achieving business objectives. Followed by, finding associated IT imperatives to can help the business realize the targeted outcomes. Technology analysis is across multiple dimensions like enterprise architecture, application portfolio, governance, process infrastructure, and security. Here also, analysis is a two-stage process, first an extension of the business analysis to the IT imperatives to validate the established linkages. Secondly, dimension specific frameworks are used for evaluating solution options and arriving at recommendations. Organization analysis is pre-dominantly a people analysis, the profile of the executive, the position they hold, and the culture of the organization as a whole. Parameters considered are organization models, decision making styles, and responsibility vs accountability.

Design Thinking is absolutely relevant for analysis & findings as it necessitates recognizing the ambiguity of the current state and diversity of the possible ways in which the target state can be defined. Characteristics of design thinking that can enhance the gap analysis are collaboration in brainstorming new ideas and grouping ideas and co-creating solutions by grouping information and exploring all possible solutions to multi-dimensional complex problems.

In this chapter, Design Thinking as applied to the Analysis & Findings phase of consulting is explained, starting with an overview of the consulting phase with illustrations for activities across consulting segments, leading to the customization of the Design Grid by selecting relevant Principles and related Practices. These intersections are further detailed as to how they can enable analysis & findings, including instantiations for select segments of the consulting spectrum.

Analysis & Findings

Objectives

The objective of the Analysis & Findings[20] phase is to analyze insights from current state assessment and gaps with regard to the defined target state and evaluate solution options. Analysis should span across the scope of the engagement, the core consulting segment, and also the corollary consulting segments, to ensure that the findings are holistic and form a firm basis for recommendations.

A simple but powerful representation of the gaps is Spider Web. Findings in one dimension are further validated across dimensions to ensure that there are only positive synergies and no negative impacts. The majority of the work in this phase is carried out by the consultants, reaching out on a need basis to the respective stakeholders for validating the analysis and the executive sponsor to playback the findings.

Key Activities

Organization & Governance Analysis

Organization analysis is pre-dominantly people analysis, the profile of the executive, the position they hold, and the culture of the organization as a whole. Business analysis is the evaluation of financial and customer perspectives to assess revenue growth, markets, products, alliances, IT investments, and spend. Governance analysis evaluates the IT functions in the context of the firm's business drivers and assesses where they best fit in

---

20   Kancharla, M. (2016), *Consulting – A Practitioner's Perspective*, Notion Press.

the organization's operations from customer need to business requirement to IT project definition/delivery to support & maintenance. The common thread here is to keep in mind the defined target state and analyze gaps in structural, alignment, and functional options, plus business risks due to gaps in the governance structure.

ILLUSTRATIONS FOR ANALYZING ORGANIZATION & GOVERNANCE

- Analysis in IT Strategy Consulting includes measures like – business perception on value realization and return on investment from IT driven initiatives, the contribution of IT projects to performance of standardized business processes for strategic initiatives, the number of IT customers, cost per customer, cost efficiency of governance processes, delivery of IT value per employee. Most importantly customer satisfaction survey data which provides insights on how well business needs are being met and the degree of alignment between business and IT.

- Analysis in IT Governance Consulting includes parameters like governance arrangements benchmarked against industry standard data of top performers, debate on the deviations, if any, stay with the arrangement if there is context specific rationale, alternatively redefine the arrangement if the reward for change outweighs the rationale for status-quo. Once the IT functions are positioned, roles will evolve, where roles don't have a natural fit, explore the possibility of a committee. Analyze – customer measures like the level of service delivery, to measure customer satisfaction, responsibility, and accountability to empower process owners to make decisions and take actions, skills, and competency development to demonstrate continuous improvement in personal.

ENTERPRISE ARCHITECTURE ANALYSIS

Enterprise architecture analysis comprehensively covers all four architecture layers. In business architecture analysis, the focus is on activities, participants, location, timing, and data/meta-data of business processes. In application architecture analysis, the focus is primarily on the business/technology linkages. In analyzing the findings of the information architecture gaps, the focus is on structure and semantics, storage and retrieval of information, with emphasis on data integrity. In analyzing the findings of the technical architecture gaps, the focus is on the configuration and control mechanisms of the infrastructure components.

ILLUSTRATIONS FOR ANALYZING ENTERPRISE ARCHITECTURE

- Business architecture – analyze activities required to accomplish the business process, frequency of usage, the current level of maturity, changes required to support the enhanced business process, participants required to accomplish the above activities, could be primary or secondary, location of activities, client-site, near-site, off-site or offshore, timing of the activities, elapse time for the complete business process, including idle times between activities, data, including meta-data of information requested for and displayed on the various presentation layers.

- Application architecture – analyze the relationships between business components vs business processes, business components vs application components, business processes vs application processes, business processes vs stakeholders, and stakeholders vs capabilities. Analyze the strategic and operational characteristics of the IT organization, availability, and associated skills of the required stakeholders.

- Information architecture – analyze complexity and criticality of information to the business in terms of quantum of data that is required in real-time and quality of data provided. Quantum of data is typically expressed in terms of nature and frequency of business intelligence that is requested by the business. Quality of data is typically expressed in terms of data privacy enforced either by internal rule-engines or external regulatory bodies, which helps in specifications for data masking.

- Technical architecture – analyze data center capabilities, domain platforms for sites/networking/delivery channels, systems management and security policies, the suitability of centralized or decentralized infrastructures for data centers and sites, environments available for application development, test, and production, security policies for business-to-business transactions and business-to-customer transactions.

Portfolio & Process Analysis

Portfolio analysis is a very rigorous and iterative exercise, typically comprising of variate analysis and overlap analysis. Variate analysis which is at the application level is a combination of univariate analysis – analysis of individual attributes, bi-variate analysis – analysis of related attributes, and multi-variate analysis – analysis combining one or more of the attributes. Overlap analysis on the other hand is between applications or combinations of applications, to relatively assess the strategic value, business value, and technical value to create the final application disposition, whether to retire, re-engineer, renovate or retain. Process analysis, on the other hand, is an in-depth analysis of the practice areas of the selected generic and specific process areas, the current capability levels, maturity levels, and a prioritized set of initiatives to bridge the gap to achieve the defined target state in case of the process of improvement and strategies to reduce waste in case of process optimization.

Illustrations for Analyzing Portfolio & Process

- In IT Portfolio Management – Functionality analysis includes univariate analysis of the strategic alignment, business value scores, and bi-variate analysis of mapping between strategic alignment and business value, strategic alignment and risk, business criticality, and risk. Technology analysis includes uni-variate analysis of the technical value, operational health scores, bi-variate analysis of mapping between business value and technical value, business criticality and technical value, technical value and operational health, and multi-variate analysis between strategic alignment, business value, and technical value. Investment analysis includes investments analysis [i.e] distribution as per the asset classes including benchmark analysis, preferably with data for the last three years, cost analysis which is essential to understand savings potentials and possible governance actions, and risk analysis to establish the risk-returns profiles of the IT portfolio.

- In IT Process Consulting the analysis is on process improvement or process optimization. Process improvement analysis is a measurement of generic practices against the generic goals applicable to the targeted maturity level and measurement of specific practices against the corresponding specific goals of the selected generic and/or specific process areas, the emphasis is on process adherence, ways to measure the extent to which the process is being followed. Key parameters for analysis are enterprise process ownership the absence of which will result in multiple solutions for similar business processes across various segments, policies standards, and procedures, they enable improvement and management. In process optimization, the emphasis is on process effectiveness, ways to measure how effectively the process meets its objectives and process efficiency, ways to measure productivity and costs around process activities.

Assets & Location Analysis

Asset analysis equates to a thorough assessment of the infrastructure components to fully understand the impact of any change if any and their implications on operations, technology, and business by looking at causes for deviation in utilization thresholds, variation in spending, and leveraging findings to define strategies for optimization. Location analysis equates to evaluating the impact to the retained organization triggered by outsourcing and implementing the target operating model. Analysis should translate to options for the new organization structure and operating model, highlighting strengths and strategies to contain weaknesses plus a high-level business case of the outsourcing model.

Illustrations for Analyzing Assets & Location

- In IT Infrastructure Consulting, analysis is about ways to improve utilization to enable reduction of physical equipment or redistribution of workload or a mix of both. The proposed infrastructure changes are run past impacted business/application owners prior to formulating the migration plan. Secondly, to improve spend, sourcing strategy, pricing models, converting capital expenditure to operating expenditure, restructuring annual maintenance contracts, redistributing suppliers, reallocating funding are analyzed. Lastly, to optimize infrastructure initiatives such as virtualization, standardization, consolidation, architectural changes, or a mix of these are analyzed.
- In IT Outsourcing Consulting, the focus of analysis is on the integrity of the interfacing units [i.e.] validation of the vendor management

processes, monitoring of metrics defined in the service level agreement, and rigor of the knowledge transfer process. In shared services analysis, proofs of concept are designed for critical and complex IT services and piloted within the shared services center. In the captive center analysis, the focus on how much the local service provider acting as guide/mentor can help in setting up and operationalizing the unit and what should be the transition strategy for a smooth handover.

OPERATING MODEL ANALYSIS

Operating model analysis is more of a cross functional analysis of the above dimensions and accordingly baselining requirements for program management, change management, and risk management.

ILLUSTRATIONS FOR ANALYZING OPERATING MODEL

- In IT Outsourcing Consulting, operating model analysis computing indices like the readiness index, suitability index, and outsource-ability index. The readiness index is a function of organizational readiness, and the suitability index is a function of technical suitability, while the outsource-ability index is a function of business criticality. These indices individually and/or collectively can determine what to outsource and in what sequence, based on which a suitable operating model for the retained organization is recommended.

- In IT Transformation Consulting, in addition to analysis of applicable consulting segments, operating model analysis focuses on program management, change management, and risk management. The analysis here involves assessment of – effective program management practices that drive clarity and consensus related to transformation initiatives, business changes at a role or even individual level so that change activities can be focused to be more effective and determination of controls to bring risks to acceptable levels.

OUTCOMES

The outcome of this phase is the third interim deliverable, a summary of analysis and inference to the findings. The deliverable is a collection of outputs of the respective frameworks with notes on inferences and dependencies that includes analysis of – gaps in business/IT alignment, architecture components, in-depth analysis of the application portfolio/processes, deviations in infrastructure utilization, options for the new organization structure/operating model leading to prioritized transformation initiatives across segments of the spectrum supported by business cases.

Opportunity for Design Thinking

In analysis & findings, hour-glass analytics come into play [i.e.] analyzing convergent insights from current state assessment and finding divergent innovations to achieve the target state definition. In a conventional approach, analysis & findings are pre-dominantly about point solutions that can bridge the existing gap. Design thinking principles and practices on the other hand acknowledge ambiguity, embrace diversity and encourage co-creation of solutions by analyzing possibilities for scale and finding synergies with other solutions in order to ensure that the transformation is sustainable.

Design Thinking in Analysis & Findings

The Algorithm for Analysis & Findings is built on the Design Thinking Principles of Embrace Ambiguity & Diversity and Co-Create Impactful Solutions.

Embrace Ambiguity & Diversity

In analysis & findings, the focus is on both ambiguity and diversity elements of the design thinking principle. One leads to the other, analyzing ambiguities of the gaps and finding diverse ways to bridge gaps. In analysis & findings both are real and required – the former tables multiplicity of parameters for consideration in finding solutions, while the latter forces the solution analyzed to be acceptable to a diversity of situations and stakeholders. Here lies the paradox, the principle is both supplementary and complementary and therefore requires a deft application.

Design thinking practices that are related to embracing ambiguity & diversity and required for analysis & findings are Brainstorming and Raskar's Hexagon.

Design Thinking in Analysis and Findings

Table 9-1: Design Grid for Analysis & Findings

	Human-centered Design	Embrace Ambiguity & Diversity	Openness to Radical Collaboration	Co-Create Impactful Solutions	Implement & Iteratively Improvise
Empathy Maps	■				
User Personas	■	■			■
How Might We			■		
Storyboarding	■		■		
Interviewing Techniques		■	■		
Brainstorming		▲	■		
Business Model Canvas		■			
Journey Maps					■
Affinity Diagrams			■	▲	
Raskar's Hexagon		▲	■		
Morphological Analysis				▲	
Value Proposition Canvas	■				

Brainstorming

Brainstorming is equally applicable to analysis & findings; multiple minds will ensure that the analysis is mutually exclusive and findings to be collectively exhaustive. Leveraging the design thinking principle of embracing ambiguity and diversity, the practice of brainstorming facilitates ideas on analyzing the real gap and finding the right solution to bridge the gap in a collaborative way with active participation from diverse stakeholders.

1. INSTANTIATION OF BRAINSTORMING FOR IT PORTFOLIO MANAGEMENT

   In IT Portfolio Management, as mentioned earlier application rationalization is the most common scope element. Application owners tend to be protective of the respective portfolio, strongly recommending the status quo, so as to not alter the profile of their respective business units.

   Conventional consulting analyzes applications independently with respective application owners and taking decisions to retain, re-engineer or retire based on the technological viability into the future, required investments in resources, and cost of maintenance. Design thinking principles through practices like brainstorming strongly advocate comprehensive analysis of application portfolios to find synergies to optimally address business needs and stretch application life making the best use of technological advancements and alternate platforms.

   Critical to the success of such brainstorming sessions are, being open minded allowing ideas to flow freely, encouraging radical thinking yet being focused, allowing collaboration, building on ideas with every stakeholder stepping-up.

2. INSTANTIATION OF BRAINSTORMING FOR IT OUTSOURCING CONSULTING

   Analysis & findings in IT Outsourcing Consulting, like in IT Portfolio Management is centered around the application portfolio and/or the infrastructure environment. In addition to all the analysis prescribed for portfolio management, outsourcing analysis extends to analysis of operational infrastructure and supporting resource model in-house as well as third party service providers.

Design Thinking in Analysis and Findings

In IT Outsourcing Consulting, analysis conventionally looks at – 1] Organizational readiness, determined by sourcing experience, resource profile, breadth and depth of technical skills, 2] Technical readiness, determined by architecture design and standards, the stability of the environment, age of application portfolio and documentation, 3] Governance readiness, determined by business/IT alignment, portfolio and project management maturity, risk management, vendor management and communication effectiveness, 4] Functional suitability, determined based on business user support, customer interaction, demand management, demand volatility, release management, time to market and vendor support and 5] Application stability, determined by the availability of application and frequency of changes, application size, and complexity. The above measures are rated individually and weighted to determine the outsource-ability index, which is then analyzed in combination to determine the transition complexity band which in turn helps to decide the transition schedule for that application.

While the above approach is comprehensive, it's still technical. The design thinking practice of brainstorming applied rightly brings in the all-important human element of analysis to outsourcing. Analyzing questions like – what happens to the internal workforce impacted by outsourcing? How do application owners cope with reduced responsibilities? Findings from such brainstorming sessions help in arriving at outsourcing strategies that can survive beyond transition.

Brainstorming at this stage, effectively tables together with the internal analysis of the current state, requirements of target state and findings of gaps to the bridge, plus the external industry/business perspectives and best practices from consultants to debate, discuss meaningfully and direct the way forward.

Raskar's Hexagon

In analysis & findings, every finding needs to be analyzed from a given premise and then extend to include all its peripheral implications. Hence the relevance of the design thinking principle embracing ambiguity & diversity. Raskar's Hexagon is lockstep in this approach as it propagates the notion of starting with an idea or solution and validating the same across multiple dimensions.

1. **INSTANTIATION OF RASKAR'S HEXAGON FOR IT ARCHITECTURE CONSULTING**

   In IT Architecture Consulting, the focus is on designing future ready software systems, the challenge lies in gauging future scenarios based on the current situation. In conventional consulting, the analysis would explore solutions – looking at the current problem or evaluating the gap with respect to the planned target state.

   Inherently the above approach is discrete, design thinking practices like Raskar's Hexagon allow for analysis to be continuous to cover all possible combinations for any given discrete solution. Consider a scenario, wherein the enterprise needs to extend its applications from accepting simple text inputs to other forms of communication.

   1. $X^{\wedge}d$ the starting point, extend the design to the next dimension. Can the system accept speech or a video along with the text?
   2. $X+Y$ the contrasting idea, a fusion of the design with a dissimilar design. Can the system extract the required text on its own or take the text from another source?
   3. X in a way doing exactly the opposite. Can the system do the required processing without any text input?
   4. $X\uparrow$ in ideating directly, given a hammer find all nails. Where else can this system be deployed?
   5. $X\downarrow$ ideating on alternatives, given a nail, find all hammers. What else can this system solve?
   6. $X++$ adding an adjective to the idea, make it faster better cheaper. How can we make the system more efficient and effective?

2. **INSTANTIATION OF RASKAR'S HEXAGON FOR IT INFRASTRUCTURE CONSULTING**

   In IT Infrastructure Consulting, the focus is on designing scalable and sustainable infrastructure, especially when there are fundamentally different

Design Thinking in Analysis and Findings

choices available for IT infrastructure. The load on IT infrastructure is increasing exponentially year after year, due to growing data and changing business needs. Decisions made on IT infrastructure have a long-lasting impact on business, hence the choice needs to be carefully assessed from all future possibilities.

In conventional consulting, the analysis would center around ways to enhance capacity or altering configurations or negotiating service level agreements/operating level agreements, pretty much technical adjustments to meet business demands. Design thinking practice, on the other hand, focuses on the ambiguity of estimating data needs and the diversity of its impact internally related to the enterprise business or externally to the industry regulations. Consider a scenario wherein, the IT infrastructure decision of whether to switch to Software as a Service [SaaS] model for the organization's CRM application?

1. X^d the starting point, extend the design to the next dimension. Can we consider any other application related to CRM for software as a service model, like Customer Engagement Management?

2. X+Y the contrasting idea, a fusion of the design with a dissimilar design. Can a portion of CRM be on 'as-a-service' model along with a portion on premise? Can a hybrid model be an option?

3. X̄ in a way doing exactly the opposite. What if we avoid 'as-a-service' model and instead strengthen our existing CRM application?

4. X↑ in ideating directly, given a hammer find all nails. Where else can 'as-a-service' model be deployed? Payroll processing, human resource management?

5. X↓ ideating on alternatives, given a nail, find all hammers. Can downstream application also be considered for 'as-a-service' model? Like billing, invoicing, etc.?

6. X++ adding an adjective to the idea. What else can be done to make the CRM application lighter, faster and cheaper?

In the process, organizations can – channel their energy towards value adding options – the complementary and combinatory ideas or exercise caution against non-value adding options – the contrasting ideas if they are not worth enriching beyond a point.

Co-Create Impactful Solutions

The creation of solutions starts in the analysis & findings phase, rather than articulating solutions in isolation if all stakeholders are brought together to co-create the solution, the chances of it being impactful are higher. Reason being, the principal factors in the all-important emotional element to prepare stakeholders for change in a participative way thereby fostering a sense of belonging and buy-in to the co-created solution. The solution itself is an outcome of the in-depth expertise of the diverse stakeholders, each respecting and honoring the strategic directives for the enterprise. The beauty of design thinking is at play at its best here, each stakeholder dynamically adapts to the role of a contributor, observer, or decision maker depending upon the finding/subject of analysis.

Design thinking practices that are related to co-creating impactful solutions and required for analysis & findings are Affinity Diagrams and Morphological Analysis.

Affinity Diagrams

Affinity diagrams help greatly in analyzing and synthesizing observations. One of the most common methods of analysis is thematic analysis. Here consultants aim to make sense of all their notes and observations by creating themes to further analyze and evaluate the findings. A feature inherent in affinity diagrams, creating groups and themes from information gathered; in the context of analysis & findings, it would be insights from an assessment of the current state, definition of the target state, and analysis of gaps.

1. **Instantiation of Affinity Diagrams for IT Strategy Consulting**

    In IT Strategy Consulting, the focus of analysis & findings is on Business IT alignment and value created by the IT investments. Ideas generated in the previous phase on ways to define the target state are now analyzed to find patterns and/or themes.

Conventional consulting focuses purely on the gaps between the current state to target state to generate a list of IT initiatives list with required investments and potential value. While these are efficient ways of conducting analysis, design thinking and practices like affinity diagrams nicely organize findings into themes and value which would resonate well with the business community.

Consider the scenario of analysis of the value created by the IT investments, this would require analysis of various financial models, based on 'what-if' scenarios to justify the return on investments. Using affinity diagrams the focus is shifted from bridging gaps, into synthesizing insights from ideas into themes, affinity diagrams also identify potential hidden and unexplored values as the stakeholder's base increases and the emotions expand during the co-creation exercise. Collectively the approach enables analysis for value at scale.

2. INSTANTIATION OF AFFINITY DIAGRAMS FOR IT PORTFOLIO MANAGEMENT

In IT Portfolio Management, the focus of analysis & findings is on performing univariate/multivariate analysis of the application portfolio and the underlying infrastructure. The goal is to ensure that they are aligned to the business, technologically relevant, and continue to have the potential to generate business value.

In conventional consulting, portfolio analysis performed is the predominantly univariate analysis of quantitative data or at best bivariate analysis to measure the degree of strategic alignment between business and IT. The extension required is qualitative analysis to find connections between application features, infrastructure configurations, cost and value of the portfolio, and expectations of stakeholders.

Consider a scenario of application portfolio analysis where-in the objective is to analyze the degree of alignment of applications landscape to the business requirements. Affinity diagrams by virtue of their focus on qualitative analysis help find intuitive connections between applications; supplemented with stakeholder needs, key performance indicators, the resulting business themes can foster a greater degree of alignment between business and IT.

The benefit of affinity diagrams as a design thinking practice lies in its ability to structurally analyze qualitative data. Starting with one data point affinity diagram helps in - finding related data points, identifying themes/patterns to perform collective analysis, that can then be summarized and synthesized into solutions.

Morphological Analysis

Morphological Analysis is a creative problem-solving technique for systematically structuring and exploring all possible solutions. Irrespective of the best of efforts and the leveraged best practices, consulting solutions seldom zero down on one solution. In co-creating impactful solutions, the practice of morphological analysis focuses on this specific aspect, the possibility of multiple solutions, which happens to be quite common in the analysis & findings phase. Leveraging morphological practice, the larger problem at hand can be broken down into its core pain points and potential impact to arrive at solution options.

1. ### Instantiation of Morphological Analysis for IT Process Consulting

    In IT Process Consulting, the focus of analysis is on end-to-end business processes and findings from maturity of supporting IT processes. Rather than analyzing the business process as a whole, better results yield when the evaluation takes place at a sub-process level, a classic case of sum or parts being more than the whole.

    Conventionally, analysis happens at a unit level to understand the flow, assessing the maturity and ability to meet service levels. While this approach works for mature organizations with defined processes, it falls short when taken to larger enterprises with complex interlinked processes, having external interfaces, and requiring adherence to regulatory stipulations.

    Morphological analysis can be a very effective innovation tool for analysis & findings in IT Process Consulting, it breaks down complex processes into sub-process and focuses on generating multiple ideas at the sub-process level and then explore combinations to improvise the business process as a whole.

Consider a business process that consists of five steps, wherein each step is validating user credentials in completely different ways. In this case, the morphological analysis will help break down the process into smaller components and identify 'user credential validation' and explore ideas for innovation at the sub-component level. In this example, the variation can be addressed in multiple ways or can be completely eliminated from one or more of the process steps.

2. INSTANTIATION OF MORPHOLOGICAL ANALYSIS FOR IT INFRASTRUCTURE CONSULTING

In IT Infrastructure Consulting, the focus of analysis is on individual infrastructure components, their capacity, configuration, and performance. Any initiative to improve utilization of infrastructure either results in the reduction of physical equipment or redistribution of workload or a mix of both.

In conventional consulting, infrastructure is optimized by virtualization, standardization, consolidation, architectural changes, or a mix of such initiatives. While this approach works well if optimization is contained with existing infrastructure, the challenge arises when optimization leads to a new technology landscape, supported by a new category of service providers. The morphological analysis comes in handy as a problem-solving method for evaluating such scenarios, taking the new or unknown and breaking it into smaller components to analyze and resolve.

Consider a scenario where a digital platform is being launched, to start with it is hard to predict – how the platform will be received by various stakeholders and customers, how it will hold up post-implementation against external factors like power outages, environmental factors like heat, humidity. In such a situation morphological analysis can play a winning role by evaluating the best fit between infrastructure and individual needs. Customers are logically grouped based on demography, domicile and the platforms can be tested for functioning and fulfillment within these smaller domains.

The value of morphological analysis is that it can help visualize multiple processes holistically and explore possibilities of combining, optimizing, reusing processes, or even retiring one or more processes. All such possibilities get formally identified and evaluated as a part of the morphological analysis to arrive at the optimal solution.

Outcomes of Design Thinking

The instantiations above amply demonstrate how the principles and practices of design thinking focus more on the third dimension, the people aspect as opposed to restricting analysis on process and technology. At the heart of any enterprise, even in a technical function like IT, the human element needs to be understood and addressed. Learnings from understanding the real drivers from real stakeholders, findings from current state assessment, definitions of target state are tabled and taken forward to evaluate solution options. The analysis is holistic, convergent analysis based on a logical grouping of findings and divergent analysis driven by breaking up findings to discover solutions that address immediate needs and also to explore adjacent and/or alternative solutions. Design thinking enables and encourages multi-faceted analysis, which is why such solutions are sustainable.

Key Learnings

In analysis & findings, the work done till date on the engagement is brought together to analyze assessment of the current state, definition of target state, and findings on the gaps between the current and future state. Analysis should span across the scope of the engagement, the core consulting segment, and also the corollary consulting segments, to ensure that the findings are holistic and form a firm basis for recommendations.

The analysis is carried out comprehensively across the dimensions of organization, governance, enterprise architecture, portfolio & process, assets & locations, and operating model. Organization analysis is pre-dominantly people analysis, the profile of the executive, the position they hold, and the culture of the organization as a whole. Governance analysis evaluates the IT functions in the context of the firm's business drivers and assesses where they best fit in the organization. Enterprise architecture analysis comprehensively covers all the four architecture layers – Focusing on the meta-data of business processes, business/technology linkages, and configuration and control mechanisms of the infrastructure components. Portfolio analysis is at the application level, individually and in combination with other applications to analyze retirement, re-engineering, renovation, or retainment of each application. Process analysis, on the other hand, is an in-depth analysis of the practice areas of the selected generic and specific process areas to assess maturity levels. Asset analysis equates to a thorough assessment of the infrastructure components, location analysis equates to evaluating impact to the retained organization triggered by outsourcing and implementing the target operating model. Operating model analysis is more of a cross functional analysis of the above dimensions and accordingly baselining requirements for program management, change management, and risk management.

Design Thinking is absolutely relevant for analysis & findings as it necessitates recognizing the ambiguity of the current state and diversity of the possible ways in which the target state can be defined. Design thinking principles and practices acknowledge ambiguity, embrace diversity and encourage co-creation of solutions by analyzing possibilities for scale and finding synergies with other solutions in order to ensure that the transformation is sustainable.

Principles relevant to analysis & findings are Embrace Ambiguity & Diversity and Co-create Impactful Solutions. Understanding the inherent ambiguities in analysis and diversity of findings is critical to creating impactful solutions.

Practice related to embracing ambiguity and diversity are Brainstorming and Raskar's Hexagon. Brainstorming helps in collectively discussing findings from analysis to arrive at solution options. Raskar's hexagon extends an identified solution option to explore complementary and supplementary solutions.

Practices related to co-create impactful solutions are Affinity Diagrams and Morphological Analysis. Affinity diagrams help group findings from analysis into patterns or themes to arrive at solution options. The morphological analysis takes a given solution and breaks it down into smaller problem statements to co-create impactful solutions.

The instantiations amply demonstrate the relevance of design thinking practices holistically to analysis & findings. From articulation of diverse ideas to bridge the gaps to peg a starting solution and explore combinatorial/contrasting ideas to grouping ideas into themes to analyze solution options and taking the larger problem, breaking it, and analyzing smaller scenarios to find optimal solutions. Collectively the practices cover all dimensions, evaluating solution components and extrapolating adjacent solutions by adopting a micro as well as a macro approach to analyzing findings.

. Ω .

Chapter 10

Design Thinking in Report and Recommendations

In Report & Recommendations phase, the focus is on synthesizing solution options and recommending strategic directions that would best address the set objectives for the engagement. Each recommendation is evaluated individually to determine the importance/impact of implementation and relatedly to determine the timing of implementation.

Design Thinking is apt for report & recommendations as it brings human-centered thinking to the fore and advocates the belief of failing fast to learn faster and better. Characteristics of design thinking that can help articulate recommendations and value proposition are storytelling, user personas, and journey maps.

In this chapter, Design Thinking as applied to the Report & Recommendations phase of consulting is explained, starting with an overview of the consulting phase with illustrations for activities across consulting segments, leading to the customization of the Design Grid by selecting relevant Principles and related Practices. These intersections are further detailed as to how they can enable report & recommendations, including instantiations for select segments of the consulting spectrum.

Report & Recommendations

Objectives

The objective of the Report & Recommendations[21] phase is to prioritize findings and develop a roadmap. The structure and contents of the roadmap would depend on the consulting segment and engagement objectives.

Key Activities

Rationale for Recommendations

Each recommendation provides for a rationale that is twofold, one drawing from experience or industry best practices and the other to demonstrate how implementing the same would address the business driver or overcome limitations of the current state or achieve the target state or bridge the gaps found in the analysis. In other words, rationales are a justification for the recommendation typically in the form business case; a verbal or written proposal that defines a problem or opportunity, the solution, the cost to implement, and the benefit that will be realized.

Illustrations for Rationale for Recommendations

- In IT Strategy Consulting, the rationale for recommendations is typically in the form of the business case, wherein the investment decisions are put into a strategic context. A pre-requisite to developing an acceptable business case for any solution is an understanding of the assumptions necessary to estimate the costs and anticipate the benefits. These assumptions could be financial, business, market, commercial or organizational. Steps to develop a business case – 1]. Define cost model, 2]. Define benefit assessment model, 3] Financial Analysis and 4]. Sensitivity Analysis. Applicable techniques include Net Present Value, Return on Investment, Total Cost of Ownership, Net Cash Flow, and Payback Period.

---

21 Kancharla, M. (2016), *Consulting – A Practitioner's Perspective*, Notion Press.

- In IT Process Consulting, the rationale for recommendations is typically in the form of process improvement goals and process improvement scope. Goals are expressed in terms of the process that is prioritized for improvement, reasons as to why it is important to enhance these processes, and classifying them as short, medium, or long term. Clearly defined and expressed goals provide a foundation for formulating milestones, managing risks, keeping the initiative on track, and ensuring its success. Scope establishes boundaries of the initiative by defining the business areas, technology systems, high level requirements for data, functions, processes, and resources that are within the scope of the initiative, as well as those that are known to be out of scope for the initiative.

- In IT Infrastructure Consulting, the rationale for recommendations is typically in the form of infrastructure optimization initiatives for improving utilization and spend and providing necessary details to prioritize and make them actionable. Parameters considered for infrastructure optimization are scalability, manageability, simplicity, stability and reliability, availability, agility, and flexibility. All infrastructure optimization initiatives are prioritized, keeping in mind the client's business operations, financial constraints, and risk appetite. Qualified initiatives are socialized with all stakeholders.

Roadmap for Recommendations

Roadmap for recommendations is the most anticipated outcome of any consulting engagement. The roadmap provides possible ways of migrating towards the target state considering the business priorities, IT capabilities, and organizational readiness to change. The roadmap is typically spread over three horizons – Horizon 1 initiatives are very critical in nature and impact the current functioning of IT, require to be initiated immediately in the short-term [within 6 months], Horizon 2 initiatives are important to be started in the medium-term [6 to 18 months timeframe] as they would enable early gains for the enterprise, Horizon 3 initiatives are considered to be a low priority but important for sustenance and would need to be re-looked at on an ongoing basis. Timeframe for implementation is long-term [18 to 36 months].

ILLUSTRATIONS FOR ROADMAP FOR RECOMMENDATIONS

- In IT Architecture Consulting, the roadmap for recommendations typically is an architecture blueprint – a sequence of architecture diagrams starting with the business architecture linking to application architecture, which in turn links to the information architecture that is finally linked to the technical architecture adhering to the architecture principles and standards. The success of the blueprint lies in the strengths of the linkages. The blueprint includes recommendations to bridge gaps, solution options with advantages & disadvantages of each option, plans for realization, notes demonstrating forward integration, and also background traceability. Equally important is the architecture governance, consisting of the requisite structure and processes that enable an organization to optimally manage its investments in technology from all aspects including enterprise IT architecture, technology vendor management, emerging technologies assessment as well as identification and building technical competencies.

- In IT Transformation Consulting, the roadmap for recommendations is a series of prioritized transformation initiatives across the segments of the spectrum, also includes quick-wins, transformation management related elements. The report is developed in two parts, strategy and implementation. Transformation strategy outlines the transformation vision, strategic improvements, conceptual enterprise architecture, technology enablement, the business case for transformation initiatives, and implementation master plan. Transformation implementation elaborates on the governance structure, mechanisms, process; transformation management office setup, structure, and reporting; change impact analysis, readiness assessment, stakeholder management, communication management; risk management, risk logs, risk mitigation; performance management and benefit management.

OUTCOMES

The outcome of this phase is the final deliverable, the Engagement Report. A comprehensive compilation of the organization context, drivers, interim deliverables like the current state assessment, target state definition, analysis, and findings in general. Depending upon the consulting segment recommendation details would be, business/IT alignment, insights on investment spend and optimized distribution for sustainable growth for IT Strategy Consulting, architecture blueprint for IT Architecture Consulting, application rationalization strategy for IT Portfolio Management. In IT Process Consulting outcomes are process areas/levels with capabilities and maturity levels and for IT Governance Consulting, governance structures, styles or archetypes, mechanisms, and measures. Likewise, initiatives for improving infrastructure utilization in IT Infrastructure Consulting and organizational readiness, application/infrastructure environment, resource profile for IT Outsourcing Consulting. And in the case of IT, Transformation Consulting recommendation outcomes would be details as above of the relevant segments.

Opportunity for Design Thinking

In the report & recommendations, insights from analysis are aggregated and revisited prior to translating findings into transformational initiatives. In doing so, the key is determining the right rationale with a business case that justifies the investment required and a roadmap to implement the recommendations in the right sequence. In a conventional approach, engagements end with the consulting report, implementation of recommendations is a follow-on project invariably by a different vendor. The potential for design thinking lies in the human-centered aspects to articulating recommendations, obtaining executive buy-in through storytelling the rationale, prototyping the same as conference room pilots, and iteratively improvise.

Design Thinking in Report & Recommendations

The Algorithm for Report & Recommendations is built on the Design Thinking Principles of Implement & Iteratively Improvise and Human-centered Design.

Implement & Iteratively Improvise

Implementing solutions in consulting engagements is typically a follow-on project. In design thinking, the notion of continuous improvement is in-built

Table 10-1: Design Grid for Report & Recommendations

	Human-centered Design	Embrace Ambiguity & Diversity	Openness to Radical Collaboration	Co-Create Impactful Solutions	Implement & Iteratively Improvise
Empathy Maps	■				
User Personas	■	■			▲
How Might We			■		
Storyboarding	▲				
Interviewing Techniques		■			
Brainstorming		■	■		
Business Model Canvas		■	■		
Journey Maps					▲
Affinity Diagrams			■	■	
Raskar's Hexagon		■	■		
Morphological Analysis				■	
Value Proposition Canvas	▲				

and is inherent in every stage. However, in the context of design thinking in consulting, the principle of implement & iteratively improvise is much more applicable in report & recommendations, since the solutions start to evolve post-analysis. Implementing here implies testing the solution in closed door conference room pilots. Relevant stakeholders evaluate recommendations, to ensure that the rationale is strong and the value proposition justifies the investment. Equally important is assessing resource availability and dependencies amongst recommendations and peg the transformation initiative in the right horizon of the roadmap.

Design thinking practices that are related to implement & iteratively improvise and required for report & recommendations are User Personas and Journey Maps.

User Personas

In articulating recommendations, revisiting existing and required personas becomes important to implement and improvise on transformational initiatives. Profiles here can be for individuals or organizational entities per recommendations; some would be net new within the organization, some could be external entities. The practice guides in defining, building interfaces, functioning of the personas independently, and in collaboration to accomplish the roadmap.

1. **Instantiation of User Personas for IT Process Consulting**

    In IT Process Consulting, user personas help in extending the processes of existing personas or establishing processes of new personas in order to support new products recommended or services to be implemented.

    Consider a scenario, wherein a company intends to broaden its customer base, beyond its primary target. In order to accomplish the above goal, the conventional approach would look at ways to extend characteristics of the existing customer segment. On the other hand, in design thinking, the practice of user personas encourages independent profiling of personas for the new customer segments. Insights from these personas help in identifying differential buying behaviors, preferred channels for purchase.

Case in point, the buying behavior of millennials who prefer purchase over eCommerce channels, necessitates establishing platforms, integrating with external entities to support this customer segment. This exercise of, process changes to user persona alignment, is iterated till an optimal balance is reached between the quantum of process changes, business viability, technical feasibility, and the associated benefits.

The value of user personas as evident from the above instantiation is that they encourage re-creating personas based on recommendations and provide an opportunity to test, fail fast, and course correct. Complementing this with the principle of iterative improvement, the practice ensures that process improvements that fail to address user needs are filtered out and only those that make the most sense are carried forward for implementation.

JOURNEY MAPS

Journey maps use a story-based approach to communicate the user's experience with a product or service. A perfect follow-on to user personas, as it articulates steps in the journey for the defined profiles. Journey maps can be particularly useful to quantify the benefits and establish linkage between architectural improvements and their impact on user experience improvement. Journey maps communicate how these user experiences will change post-implementation of recommendations.

1. INSTANTIATION OF JOURNEY MAPS FOR IT ARCHITECTURE CONSULTING

   IT Architecture Consulting in the recommendations phase is all about presenting the enterprise architecture blueprint and roadmap. In order to institutionalize the same, the interchange from business architecture to the application to information to infrastructure architectures should be seamless.

Design Thinking in Report and Recommendations

Consider a scenario, wherein the objective of an online retailer is to create the best possible user experience on their site, ensuring visitors find everything they're looking for with ease and speed. In the conventional approach, the architecture is defined purely for the product in mind, seldom factoring in related products. Leveraging design thinking, the practice of journey maps traverses the steps associated with specific and related products as recommended.

Case in point, users not having the ability to access linked products, therefore having to wait for several seconds for the images to load on the site. In this case, the journey map starts with the 'Scenario' – 'a potential customer trying to access linked products', then identify the 'Actor' in the scenario, here it's the 'potential customer'. Now list the 'Actions' the potential interfaces the enterprise architecture needs to provide – compressed images, changes to information architecture to enable cross linkage of products, using dedicated content delivery network or a mix of these solutions.

The value of journey maps as evident from the above instantiation is that they help – quantify the improvement between actual user journeys and recommended user journeys, identify redundant, superfluous actions and serve as an effective tool to boost productivity and save cost. In reality, it's highly unlikely that the recommended user journeys are defined correctly in a single attempt, the principle of implement and iteratively improvising helps evaluate repercussions ranging from business, technology, process, and even architectural decisions. Journey maps can be a very effective tool to iteratively eliminate solution options and select the ones that have maximum impact on user experience.

HUMAN-CENTERED DESIGN

Human-centered design helps in articulating recommendations in such a way that the implemented solutions are sustainable. The human centric aspect encourages consultants to look beyond the hard facts from findings into the aspirations of stakeholders and ambitions of the executives. In relation to the key activities of the report & recommendations, this principle aids in storytelling the rationale for each recommendation and in demonstrating the value proposition of the business case leading to a roadmap that is practical to implement.

Design thinking practices that are related to human-centered design and required for report & recommendations are Storyboarding and Value Proposition Canvas.

STORYBOARDING

Storyboards can help the client stakeholders visualize how things are going to change and by what timeframes. Storyboarding can be applied to report & recommendations albeit in reverse order; telling recommendations as a story. Narrating the rationale, as to how the recommendations help overcome the challenges of the current state and take the enterprise closer to the target state. The visualization also opens a channel to iterate and revisit or reprioritize certain recommendations. Complementing these benefits with the voice of the customers, the storyboard drives executive buy-in and a desire to action the advice.

1. INSTANTIATION OF STORYBOARDING FOR IT INFRASTRUCTURE CONSULTING

    In IT Infrastructure Consulting, the recommendations are predominantly in the form of how investments can be optimized and/or how infrastructure can be virtualized. The associated initiatives are technically complex, yet need to be presented to a business in a simple manner.

    Consider the case of a global enterprise undergoing a multi-year transformation to consolidate its back-office operations into a single location to leverage economies of scale. Conventionally, the rationale is presented in terms of the risk of being technologically obsolete or the limited increase in operational expenditures, or the return on investment from capital expenditures. The practice of storyboarding, through storytelling simplifies the recommendation by tracing it back to insights from analysis, challenges of the current state, experiences of back-office operators.

Design Thinking in Report and Recommendations 195

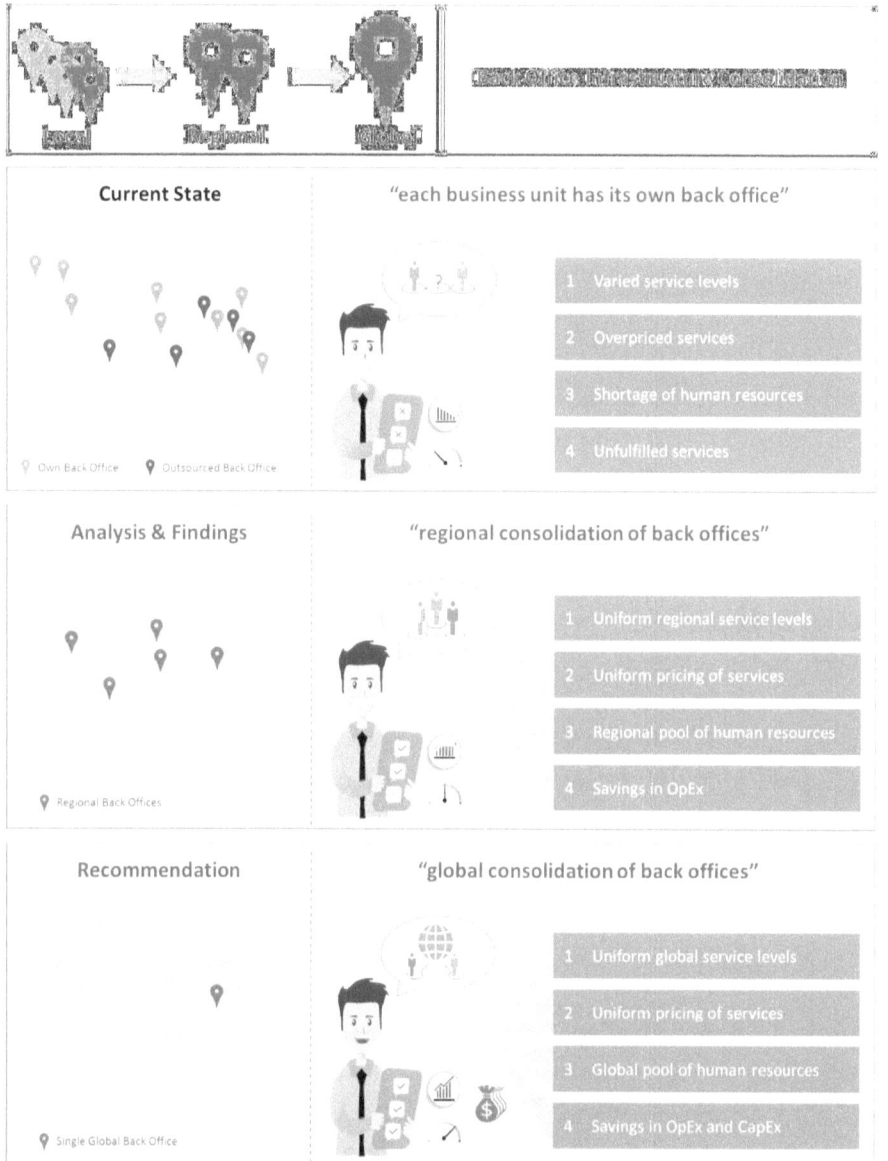

Figure 10-1: Storyboarding

Case in point, global consolidation of back-office centers as a recommendation is triggered by the various service levels in operations, overpriced services, manpower shortages, and unfulfilled services as the voice of the customer. Insights from analysis recommended a phased transition from localized back-offices to regional hubs bring in uniformity in services, price, shared manpower, and savings in operational expenditures. The recommendation will resonate better if the benefit of the recommendation is reiterated post this narrative, creates a sense of satisfaction that the recommendation is realistic and can be realized.

The advantage of storyboards is that they are, low fidelity and effective means of communicating back to stakeholders, the near-term and long-term view of business, the stages of changes, and associated benefits. Stakeholder feedback can be collected at each iteration to make changes to recommendations and roadmap as needed to ensure sustainability.

VALUE PROPOSITION CANVAS

The value proposition is the crux of every consulting report and therefore the relevance of the design thinking practice value proposition canvas to report and recommendations. Value proposition canvas goes hand in hand with business model canvas, specifically the two building blocks of value proposition and customer segments. Given the practice objective of assessing fitment between the organization's offerings and customer's needs, articulating value proposition through the principle of human-centered design, can make the recommendations a force-multiplier.

1. **INSTANTIATION OF VALUE PROPOSITION CANVAS FOR IT TRANSFORMATION CONSULTING**

    In IT Transformation Consulting, the recommendations should address all of the enterprise perspectives – organization, business, technology, process, and governance. Continuing on the scenario of the IT organization embarking on an internal digital transformation initiative to streamline its operations to support anytime/anywhere availability of their applications to their associates on any-device, the instantiation here focuses on articulating the value proposition of the recommendations.

    In the customer segment of the business model canvas, the current state assessment captured the unmet needs and the target state definition emphasized the shift required in way of working. And in the value

Design Thinking in Report and Recommendations 197

proposition segment of the business model canvas, the current state assessment baselined the platforms supported and target state definition emphasized the challenges of operationalizing the analyzed solution.

In value proposition canvas, the customer profile is first mapped in terms of his/her job, pains, and gains. Based on each customer profile value propositions are mapped to create the value map, a combination of products and services that can help customers complete their job, pain relievers, and gain creators.

Customer Profile, development teams, solution architects, industry experts, sales representatives, management executives, and the newly defined segment digital champions.

- Customer Jobs – solution architecting, software development, customer relationship management, analyst relations, managing revenues, and measuring performance.

- Customer Pains – a proliferation of siloed systems, constraints of existing technology platforms, and availability of real-time data.

- Customer Gains – applications available and accessible anywhere/anytime on any device.

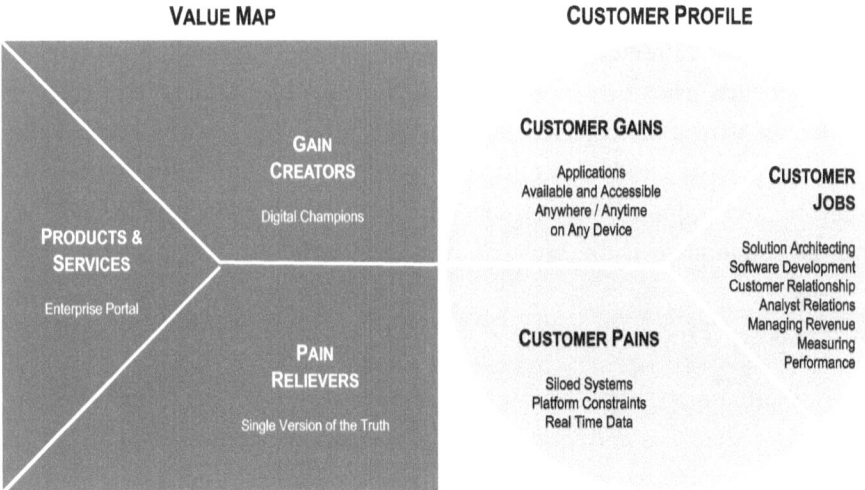

Figure 10-2: Value Proposition Canvas

Value Proposition lies in the ability of the recommendations to meet customers' unmet needs and the ease of the same. The organization's ability to change is key to success, internally with the employees, externally with clients, partners, competitors, and regulatory bodies.

- Products and Services, the enterprise portal developed as a suite of web-based applications, mobile apps and hosted on a secure cloud environment.

- Pain Relievers, digital platform with a rationalized application portfolio available across devices providing real-time data and more importantly a single version of the truth.

- Gain Creators, digital champions performing the role of data scientist, design thinker, or innovation evangelists driving change to transform the organization.

The final step in the value proposition canvas is the fitment between customer profile and value map. Elaborate upon – 1] how the platform can be capitalized by the various customer segments, 2] how to learn and leverage the skills and capabilities of data scientists, design thinkers and innovation evangelists, 3] how to make the best use of the digital platform to make the value proposition comprehensive and complete.

The benefit of value proposition canvas as a design thinking practice is that it first creates a customer profile in terms of the jobs they perform, the pains they experience, gains they aspire and match them with products, services and/or offerings that are either pain relievers or gain creators. In the instantiation above, the practice clearly demonstrates its ability to comprehensively cover the enterprise and propose recommendations for transformation that are not just practical and implementable but are human-centered.

OUTCOMES OF DESIGN THINKING

The instantiations above adequately demonstrate how the principles and practices of design thinking aid in testing recommendations. Prototyped as conference room pilots they are limited, but nonetheless, they provide critical insights to improvise and implement. The practices progressively create personas required for transformation, build process steps of the journey maps, trace rationale of recommendations to voice of the customer, and articulate value proposition for each customer segment. Collectively a dream come true for any executive sponsor of consulting engagements – to visualize the value of implementation upfront.

KEY LEARNINGS

Consulting engagements culminate with the recommendations phase. Engagement report includes context and drivers, assessment of the current state, definition of the target state, findings from analysis in summary format. Followed by details of the rationale for the recommendation, business cases with a value proposition, and roadmap for implementation, an executive summary of the same is presented to the engagement sponsor, key stakeholders.

Key activities of this phase are the rationale for recommendation covers the internal perspective of challenges, corrective measures, and external perspective of best practices that could be leveraged. Recommended initiatives are then time-lined across horizons as a roadmap for implementation.

Design Thinking is an asset in terms of its human-centered focus and an accelerator to the recommendations phase in terms of the potential to prototype, test, iterate, and improvise. Principles relevant to report & recommendations are Implement & Iteratively Improvise and Human-centered Design. The former focuses on the person and process aspects of recommendations and for the latter, the focus is on backward justification and forward value from propositions.

Practice related to implement & iteratively improvise are User Personas and Journey Maps. User personas profile the future stakeholders, resulting because of change in characteristics of existing stakeholders of creation of new characters. Journey maps peg the process steps, in ways that can maximize the impact of user experience.

Practices related to human-centered design are Storyboarding and Value Proposition Design. Storyboarding through storytelling the rationale for recommendations enables executive buy-in. Value propositions developed to address the needs of all customer segments ensure success in implementation.

The instantiations amply demonstrate the ability of design thinking – to profile personas and create platforms for new customer segments, to enhance processes to support the purchase of linked products through changes to information architecture, to story tell the rationale for infrastructure consolidation through storyboards, and to comprehensively address all of the enterprise perspectives in digital transformation through value maps for customer profiles on the value proposition canvas.

. Ω .

Bibliography

i. Brown, T. (2009), *Change by Design*, Harper Collis.

ii. Cross, N. (2011), *Design Thinking*, Bloomsbury.

iii. Google, *Design Sprint Framework*.

iv. IDEO.org (2015), *Design Kit: The Field Guide to Human-Centered Design*.

v. Kancharla, M. (2016), *Consulting – A Practitioner's Perspective*, Notion Press.

vi. Kelley, D. & Kelley, T. (2013), *Creative Confidence*, William Collins.

vii. Kelley, T. (2016), *The Art of Innovation*, Profile Books.

viii. Kelley, T. (2016), *The Ten Faces of Innovation*, Profile Books.

ix. Lockwood, T. & Papke, E. (2018), *Innovation by Design,* Career Press.

x. Martin, R. (2009), *The Design of Business*, Harvard Business Press.

xi. Norman, D. (2013), *The Design of Everyday Things*, Basic Books.

xii. Osterwalder, A. & Pigneur, Y. (2010), *Business Model Generation*, Wiley India Pvt. Ltd.

xiii. Osterwalder, A. Pigneur, Y. Bernarda, G. & Smith, A. (2014), *Value Proposition Design*, Wiley India Pvt. Ltd.

xiv. Stanford d. School, *Design Thinking bootcamp bootleg*.

End Notes

Professionally I'm a career consultant, personally, my passion lies in the creative arts. Having compiled my experiences of the former in my earlier book, my research shifted to the latter and discovered design thinking.

My heartfelt gratitude to Roger Martin, for introducing me to the 'Knowledge Funnel' in his book 'Design of Business', made a very profound impact on me and prompted me to explore possibilities of design thinking in consulting. So much so that, I have even structured my book along the stages of the knowledge funnel. Chapter 2 introduces Knowledge Funnel and Mysteries of Consulting, Chapter 3 outlines the Heuristics of Design Thinking, Chapter 4 captures his views on Design Thinking in Business, and in Chapter 5 Algorithms for Design Thinking in Consulting are articulated.

'The Art of Innovation' by Tom Kelley seeded lessons in creativity, 'The Ten Faces of Innovation' provided strategies for heightening creativity and Creative Confidence co-authored with David Kelley, unleashed my creative potential, not to forget their insights from interviews that inspired sections in Chapter 3. Tim Brown's seminal article on Design Thinking published in Harvard Business Review and his book 'Change by Design' coupled with their work at IDEO, helped define the elements of Design Thinking in Chapter 3. Equally inspired by Nigel Cross's 'Design Thinking', Don Norman's 'The Design of Everyday Things', Thomas Lockwood & Edgar Papke's 'Innovation by Design'. Information is aplenty on the internet, from Wikipedia to several other websites, published articles, research reports, analyst findings, frameworks, experiments, and experiences have been researched and redacted in Chapter 3 to chronicle and contextualize design thinking across all perspectives.

Alex Osterwalder & Yves Pigneur's 'Business Model Generation' and 'Value Proposition Design' are introduced as practices of design thinking in Chapter 4 and instantiated in Chapter 7, Chapter 8, and Chapter 10.

Last but not the least, I must acknowledge the efforts of my fellow design thinkers Avadhesh Tewari and Mohan Mallari for sparing their after-office hours in researching, reviewing, and in the reproduction of this book.

Design thinking is all about ideation and building upon them iteratively. Thanks to all the design thinking pioneers, thought leaders, authors, analysts, researchers and practitioners, institutions, associations, and organizations, referenced above and beyond, for giving me a sandbox to ideate upon, synthesizing your insights to innovate and invent the 'Design Grid' – my idea to apply 'Design Thinking in Consulting'.

Epilogue

"**Design Thinking in Consulting**" is an experimental book, an analysis of consulting in the future by applying a contemporary thought like design thinking.

Design Thinking fascinated me on a platitude of parameters, primarily its focus on customer experience and the emphasis on the human-centered approach to problem solving. Learnings from design thinking in products and services have been my compass to navigate through the unchartered territory of design thinking in consulting and creation of the 'Design Grid'; my attempt at a reality distortion field for consulting.

I thoroughly enjoyed the experience; the book rejuvenated me to think beyond the obvious and inspired me to restructure my thought process on the lines of the knowledge funnel, to find meaning in mysteries, holistically analyze heuristics and articulate algorithms for Consulting 2.0.

HOPE MY EXPERIMENT... ENRICHES YOUR EXPERIENCE!

INDEX

A

Affinity Diagrams, 90-91, 159-161, 178-180
Alexander Osterwalder, 87, 94
Alistair Fuad-Luke, 58

B

Brainstorming, 86, 136-137, 174-175
Buckminster Fuller, 54
Business Case, 20
Business Consulting, 16
Business Model Canvas, 87-88, 136-140, 155-158

C

Co-create Impactful Solutions, 80, 178
Consulting Cycle, 34-35
Consulting Space, 16
Consulting Spectrum, 18

D

David Kelley, 56-57
Design Grid, 75, 77, 78
   Design Grid for Analysis & Findings, 173
   Design Grid for Current State Assessment, 133
   Design Grid for Report & Recommendations, 190
   Design Grid for Target State Definition, 152
   Design Grid for Understanding Context, 110
Design Practices, 82
Design Principles, 79
Design Thinking Frameworks
   d-School Framework, 61-62, 64
   Google's Design Sprints, 70-71
   IDEO's Framework, 65, 67, 69
Donald Norman, 55

E

Embrace Ambiguity & Diversity, 79, 132, 151, 172
Empathy Maps, 82, 109, 111-112
Enterprise Architecture, 20-22, 161-162, 167-168, 182-183, 192-193

F

Functional Consulting, 17

H

Herbert Simon, 54
Heuristics of Design Thinking, 76-77
How Might We, 83-84, 115-117
Human-centered Design, 79, 109, 193

I

Implement & Iteratively Improvise, 81, 189
Interviewing Techniques, 85, 132, 134
Investment Analysis, 23
Investment Management, 24
IT Consulting, 17-18
  IT Architecture Consulting, 20-21, 104-105, 116, 126, 128, 146, 148, 161, 176, 188, 192
  IT Governance Consulting, 26, 105, 107-108, 111, 117, 125, 132, 145, 154, 160, 167
  IT Infrastructure Consulting, 28, 106, 108, 113, 128, 148, 170, 176, 181, 187, 194
  IT Outsourcing Consulting, 30, 107, 112, 114, 125, 134, 145, 154, 170-171, 174
  IT Portfolio Management, 22, 105-106, 116, 126, 137, 146, 160, 169, 174, 179
  IT Process Consulting, 25, 106-107, 111, 129, 135, 149, 169, 180, 187, 191
  IT Strategy Consulting, 19, 104, 113, 115, 124, 126-127, 144-145, 147, 153, 159, 167, 178, 186,
  IT Transformation Consulting, 32, 108, 117-118, 127, 137, 146, 155, 171, 188, 196

J

Journey Maps, 90, 135-136, 192

K

Knowledge Funnel, 45-47, 100

M

Morphological Analysis, 93, 180-181
Mysteries of Consulting, 47-48

N

Nigel Cross, 56

O

Openness to Radical Collaboration, 80, 114, 136, 159
Operational Consulting, 18

R

Raskar's Hexagon, 91-92, 159, 161, 175-176
Roger Martin, 45
Rolf Faste, 56, 72

S

SAPPGIO-T, 18
Storyboarding, 84, 118-119, 194-195
Strategy Consulting, 16

T

Tim Brown, 56-57
Tom Kelley, 57

U

User Personas, 83, 112-114, 153-154, 191
User-Centered Design, 55

V

Value Proposition Canvas, 94-95, 196-197

Y

Yves Pigneur, 87, 94

About the Author

Mohan Kancharla has a Bachelor's degree in Computer Engineering and a Post Graduate Diploma in Management from the Indian Institute of Management, Calcutta, with over three decades of experience in Information Technology and Consulting.

A Certified Management Consultant, his experience spans across verticals and across the consulting spectrum, having successfully directed multiple consulting engagements for Fortune 500 companies worldwide.

Mohan has published several articles on IT Strategy and Governance in leading journals, is an Invited Faculty on IT Consulting and Co-Innovator of 'Strategy Validation Framework' (Patent Pending). He is Certified in 'Innovation of Products and Services' MIT's Approach to Design Thinking, and is also a Certified Corporate Director and Certified Executive Coach.

Mohan is recognized by *CEO Today* as one of the 'Top 100 Global Management Consultants' and was awarded 'CEO Today Management Consulting Award 2018'.

Mohan lives in Chennai, India, with his wife Mary Rajeswari and daughters Kezia Harshita and Nikia Sushmita.

www.ingramcontent.com/pod-product-compliance
Lightning Source LLC
Chambersburg PA
CBHW030932180526
45163CB00002B/539